Business Automation and Its Effect on the Labor Force

Business Automation and Its Effect on the Labor Force informs business managers on new technologies that can make their industries more efficient. This book provides a primer on quantum computing, artificial intelligence, robotics, and sensors. As a business management book, managers can start planning for the future. The author predicts when the advanced systems would be ready to use. Getting a clearer picture of what is on the horizon, business managers can determine how many workers and machines will be needed. Managers will learn how to calculate the optimal mix of workers and machines.

Key Book Highlights

- Covering labor and technology in agriculture, manufacturing, construction, transportation, hospitality, health care, office administration, and education.
- A review of the evolution of systems, machines, and devices from the past to the present, and where the latest advancement is headed.
- A visual timeline showing when new systems and machines would be available for eight industries in the next 25 years.
- Succinct descriptions of eliminated jobs, retained jobs, and new roles for workers.
- A simplified method to calculate the costs of operations, allowing business managers to compare human productivity against machine productivity.
- Labor market information in context of technological innovation for state workforce agencies and local workforce development boards.
- Lists of occupations with Standard Occupational Classification (SOC) codes for labor economists, workforce development specialists, and job seekers.

Business Automation and Its Effect on the Labor Force

A Practical Guide for Preparing Organizations for the Fourth Industrial Revolution

Edward Y. Uechi

Routledge
Taylor & Francis Group

A PRODUCTIVITY PRESS BOOK

First published 2023
by Routledge
605 Third Avenue, New York, NY 10158

and by Routledge
4 Park Square, Milton Park, Abingdon, Oxon, OX14 4RN

Routledge is an imprint of the Taylor & Francis Group, an informa business

Library of Congress Cataloging-in-Publication Data
A catalog record for this book has been requested

ISBN: 978-1-03203-837-7 (hbk)
ISBN: 978-1-03203-834-6 (pbk)
ISBN: 978-1-00318-932-9 (ebk)

DOI: 10.4324/9781003189329

Typeset in Garamond
by Apex CoVantage, LLC

Contents

About the Author

Over a 25-year professional career, Edward Y. Uechi has helped people in the United States and other countries to use information technology (IT) to their advantage. After establishing his expertise in the IT field at a high-technology international corporation in Silicon Valley, he has provided training and technical assistance to government agencies and private companies. He founded and led a non-profit organization and a social enterprise. Most recently, Edward has focused on workforce development where he manages government programs and analyzes employment data.

Edward brings a combination of expertise in IT and organizational development with emphasis on business process re-engineering to advise a diverse range of organizations on IT modernization efforts. His level of guidance is marked by high practicality that allows organizations to make substantial improvements to operations with relative ease and low cost.

Edward earned a Bachelor of Arts degree in International Security and Conflict Resolution from San Diego State University and a Master of Public Administration degree from the Maxwell School of Syracuse University. Hc is the author of *Public Service Information Technology: The Definitive Manager's Guide to Harnessing Technology for Cost-Effective Operations and Services* (Routledge/Productivity Press, 2020).

Figures

Introduction

The world is undergoing a transformation that will move civilization to a new era of human endeavor. The futurist, Alvin Toffler, described where society could be headed. In *The Third Wave*, he envisioned a postindustrial period in which all of us would experience a "truly humane civilization."[1] Toffler analyzed how our species had progressed over thousands of years to remake civilization that was better and more advanced than the previous civilization. According to Toffler, the world had gone through a first wave to transform a primitive society into an agrarian society and a second wave to transform that agrarian society into an industrial society. In each case, Toffler surmised that humans needed a new form of energy, a new form of technology, and a new form of distribution in order to break away from the current system and create a new system. Jeremy Rifkin, author of *The Third Industrial Revolution*, added that a new form of communication played an equal role in the transformation. The interplay of energy, technology, distribution, and communication all working together were the essential components to move an entire society to a new economic system.

The second wave that Toffler described can be split into two industrial revolutions. The first industrial revolution, which was from 1760 to 1840 roughly speaking, is marked by the use of coal as the energy source, machines to increase production, steam-powered vehicles to distribute goods and materials, and the printing press to deliver written materials. The second industrial revolution, which spanned the second half of the 19th century into the early 20th century, is marked by the use of oil and electricity as the energy sources, mass production with a whole host of machines and methods to further increase production, vehicles powered by an internal combustion engine to distribute goods and materials, and the telephone to deliver oral messages faster than the written word. Some researchers would

DOI: 10.4324/9781003189329-1

extend the second industrial revolution longer until 1940, and such an extension would add radio and motion pictures as new communication forms.

There is no academic consensus yet on the definitive definitions of the third and fourth industrial revolutions. Literature refers to the third industrial revolution as focused on information technology (IT) that started around 1950 and continued to 2000.[2] Computers and electronics were mainly described with little discussion on the other components. It can be reasonably assumed that the defining characteristics that mark the third industrial revolution would be nuclear power as the new energy source, computers to automate production, aircraft to distribute goods and materials, satellites to relay data, and television and video to deliver information.

Based on a synthesis of multiple sources from the literature, the fourth industrial revolution (coined by Klaus Schwab, Founder and Executive Chairman of the World Economic Forum) could be marked as starting at 2000 and defined as using renewable energy sources, artificial intelligence (AI), Internet-of-Things (IoT), and quantum computing to optimize production, 3D printing to create unique objects, electric vehicles to distribute goods and materials, and the Internet to deliver information rapidly to any location around the globe. What makes this revolution distinct from the third is "[the] fusion of technologies that is blurring the lines between the physical, digital, and biological spheres."[3] Computer technologies – especially the miniaturization of electronics – are being integrated into a diverse array of objects that hitherto have not been done. And the development of such new systems and devices "is evolving at an exponential [non-linear] pace," unlike anything seen in previous revolutions.[4] Because multiple scientific disciplines are involved, technical progress is not as simple as following one particular field but observing various areas running in parallel that will converge at some point. The fourth industrial revolution has the potential of transforming all industries.

As the fourth industrial revolution plays out over the next decades, business managers would need to understand what this will all mean to their business and organization. Across all industry sectors, business managers would be able to take advantage of the latest innovations to automate their business processes. The possibilities are endless. From managing a restaurant to constructing a freeway, operations could be made more productive and less costly by employing machines instead of humans. Having little to no dependence on humans then could enable a business to produce products truly around the clock – 24 hours a day, 7 days a week.

If all companies in every industry sector choose to employ machines to automate their business, then what will happen to human workers? Can workers find jobs elsewhere?

This book (the first of a two-volume set) examines the impact that technological development will have on production, focusing specifically on how technology will change the demand for human workers. The twofold purpose of this book is (1) to explain how and when automated industries are likely to be realized and (2) to articulate the implications that would arise from widespread automation across the economy. The contents of this book will help business managers to prepare for the future – the fourth industrial revolution.

Written from the viewpoint of an IT manager who specializes in workforce development and evaluates computer-based information systems, this book provides advice that is grounded in experience. Based on the development of the underlying technologies and other factors, I make forecasts on when certain technological systems will be available for implementation. The prediction looks out 25 years to 2046. I further make determinations on which occupations could be affected by business automation. Jobs that can be replaced by machines are identified.

A critical need at this time is to identify the jobs that would be lost and the jobs that would be retained. Not all human jobs will be eliminated. New jobs will form. This book provides descriptions of what new jobs could result, so that workers can be informed about emerging opportunities.

Another critical need is to calm the anxieties that people may have regarding emerging technologies, especially AI as it is implemented in a machine to create a human-like robot. The rapid development of computer engineering in the last 25 years has captured the popular imagination in ways that have excited many of the possibilities and have also evoked a great amount of fear of what may or may not come true. With a technical review of the technologies, this book provides a realistic view of where technological development is heading toward and in so doing can allow for a sensible discussion on the effects of automation.

The structure of this book was designed in a way where a business manager does not have to read the entire book. The business manager can read the first two chapters, select the specific industry chapter that the manager works in between Chapters 3 and 10, and finally read the last two chapters. Chapters 3–10 cover a specific industry sector, agriculture, manufacturing, construction, transportation and warehousing, accommodation and food services, health care, administrative and support, and educational services, respectively. Unless the manager works in all industries, the business manager does not have to read all chapters. The business manager can get all the necessary information by reading a total of five chapters.

Workers and job seekers can start by reading Chapters 11 and 12 and then focus on the last sections in Chapters 3–10. There the worker will find lists of occupations of interest to review.

Policymakers and the general public can just read Chapters 2, 11, and 12. Further details on any particular topic can be followed up on, as desired, by reading any one of the other chapters.

The chapters are summarized as follows:

Chapter 1 introduces the economics of production, emphasizing on the analysis of all available resources that will go into producing a good or service. A new and straightforward equation is proposed to analyze production in any business.

Chapter 2 explains the development of technologies, starting with the computer and moving on to how the computer and electronic parts have been integrated into machines and the human body. Recent research in electrical engineering, mechanical engineering, nanotechnology, and biology highlights advancements.

Chapters 3–10 follow a standard outline to describe a specific industry sector, the demand for human workers, the past and future technological systems, a forecast of future systems, and the occupations that would be affected and unaffected by automation. Chapter 9 is an exception where adjustments were made to the standard outline. The content in each of Chapters 3–10 is relevant to a specific industry sector.

Chapter 11 summarizes the technological systems described in the preceding eight chapters to find similarities that systems share across multiple industries. The forecasts of when systems would be implemented are analyzed to create a composite view of eight industry sectors. A timeline of all sectors in one view illustrates those sectors that would automate sooner and those sectors that would automate later.

Chapter 12 describes the effect that automation will have on the labor force, summarizing all of the lost jobs and all of the new jobs identified in Chapters 3–10. The differences between the new jobs and the lost jobs are analyzed to identify the skills and abilities that workers will need to transition to new occupations. Given what has been explained in previous chapters, the production equation is revisited to explain the use of the equation to find combinations of labor and machine inputs that would be optimal for a particular organization. The explanation of the production equation leads into a discussion of the implications that widespread automation across the economy could have for the labor force.

Notes are organized by chapters and can be found at the end of the chapters. Source materials are listed in a bibliography at the end of the book. A diverse mix of sources include government reports, academic articles, trade articles, consumer articles, and patent invention specifications.

All of the labor data spread across from Chapter 3 to Chapter 12 come from one source. The data set is the May 2019 Occupational Employment Statistics survey from the U.S. Bureau of Labor Statistics. To avoid any confounding effect with the Coronavirus (COVID-19) pandemic, it was decided to use the last data set that was collected before the onset of the pandemic. The May 2019 data represent employment numbers that were not affected by the pandemic.

The next book that will complete the two-volume set will explore public policies to address the implications touched upon in the last chapter. Policy solutions will be examined to solve the dilemma of permanently unemployed workers, which could result from the effect of widespread business automation.

Notes

1 Alvin Toffler (1980) *The Third Wave* (New York: Bantam Books), p. 10 in the Kindle version.
2 Jeremy Rifkin, author of *The Third Industrial Revolution*.
3 Klaus Schwab (2016) "The Fourth Industrial Revolution: What It Means, How to Respond," 14 January, *World Economic Forum*. <https://www.weforum.org/agenda/2016/01/the-fourth-industrial-revolution-what-it-means-and-how-to-respond/?msclkid=0e3d7183bc9911ecbbbb6bc287a4a74d>
4 Schwab.

Chapter 1

Cost and Use of Resources

1.1 Chapter Summary

Chapter 1 introduces the economics of production, emphasizing on the analysis of all available resources that will go into producing a good or service. I review the Cobb–Douglas production function and how it has been improved over the years. A new and straightforward equation is proposed to analyze production in any business. This new production equation is explained with a few operating scenarios to serve as examples. The chapter concludes with three theoretical scenarios that serve as reference points for organizations to use as they find the right mix of hiring human workers and implementing machines.

1.2 Operations and Resources

How an organization carries out operations to produce a good or service depends on the resources that it will use. Resources can come in all sorts, human labor, machinery, tools, raw and manufactured materials, facilities, and land. Any combination of resources will contribute to the production of a good. A critical task then is on deciding what combination would be optimal to produce the maximum possible units of a good.

The choice of resources is critical because an inadequate combination might result in producing an amount that does not fully meet consumer demand. A combination that was not well planned might lead to spending more money than an organization has to.

DOI: 10.4324/9781003189329-2

Each type of resource has a cost. Workers need to be paid. Machines have to be paid for. Materials and other resources have to purchased. The sum of all the chosen resources will add up. Unless an organization has all the money it needs, the organization would not be able to use all possible resources. Even if all available funds were available, using all resources may not be efficient. The organization, therefore, has to evaluate not only the type of resource but both the type and cost of the resource. The right combination must be economical that allows the organization to produce its target quantity of goods at the lowest possible cost.

What is the right combination?

There really is no right or wrong combination of resources. What one organization in one industry chooses can be quite different from another organization in another industry. Even within the same industry, two organizations can have different combinations. In some cases, that combination can be tightly held by a particular organization to be a trade secret. This would be true in a highly competitive industry that has numerous organizations competing for the same customers. In a competitive market, an organization with the most cost-effective production could take most of the customers away from its competitors that operate with less optimal and less efficient operations.

How can a combination of resources be found? Is there a formula?

Charles Cobb and Paul Douglas developed their production function that has been widely used for decades in calculating total output and for providing a way to explain economic growth or decline. The Cobb–Douglas production function makes an approximation of total output based on the amounts of labor and capital used in industry sectors. Capital is referred to as equipment, tools, and buildings. Raw materials, goods, and supplies that are used directly in production can also be included as capital. Cobb and Douglas developed their equation based on a theory that "production, labor, and capital are so related that if [one] multiplies both labor and capital by a factor *m*, then production will be increased *m* times."[1]

The Cobb–Douglas production function tends to be biased toward labor, however. In the equation, more weight is given to labor than what is given to capital. The formula suggests that capital does not contribute to production equally to the contribution of labor. The weighted value applied to capital is significantly less than that applied to labor. This would have made sense when Cobb and Douglas had published their formula in 1928. For centuries, human labor was the dominant means to produce goods. Although advances in technology were made from the late 19th century to early 20th century, the amount of data related to capital was not fully collected and analyzed, if not fully appreciated. Production data relied on wages and workers.

Cobb and Douglas understood the issues in devising an equation to explain production. They never claimed to have perfected a formula, but proposed a method that can be improved upon. Cobb and Douglas concluded that more work was needed to analyze production. The scope of this book focuses on two of the four areas that Cobb and Douglas identified for improvement. The two areas are:

> (1) [Improving the] index of labor supply which will approximate more closely the relative actual number of hours worked not only by manual workers but also by clerical workers as well and (2) [Creating] a better index of capital growth.[2]

Robert Solow analyzed the role of capital in the Cobb–Douglas production function and stressed that "what belongs in a production function is *capital in use*, not capital in place [emphasis added]."[3] When analyzing the types of capital, one needs to distinguish between capital that directly contributes to the manufacture of a good and capital that does not contribute anything to the manufacture of a good. A type of capital can sit idle doing nothing on the factory floor. Another type of capital can simply exist but can have little to no logical connection to the actual making of a product. A building, for example, provides protection for workers and machines, but does the building contribute to the making of a product?

Formal terminology differentiates types of capital between fixed capital and working capital. Working capital such as raw materials and supplies can be factored in production if they directly contribute to the manufacture of a good. Some types of fixed capital such as machines and tools that had been purchased to manufacture a good can also be factored in production. Whether it is fixed capital or working capital, the capital resource needs to have a logical connection to the making of a good or service for it to be included in the production function.

Not including applicable capital resources could lead to an inaccurate estimate of production, if not a misleading view of production. Baptist and Hepburn measured the factors of labor, capital, and materials across several industry sectors that rely on natural resources and raw materials (e.g., textile, petroleum, paper manufacturing, and furniture manufacturing). They found that excluding raw materials out of the equation could overstate total output in resource-intensive industries.[4]

An important point is to determine whether or not capital is being utilized in production. Labor is well understood in this regard. Human workers are employed to do particular jobs in production. Thus, human workers are being utilized in production. Likewise, various types of capital can be employed to do particular jobs in production. Therefore, various types of capital can be utilized in production.

In terms of measuring capital, Paul Romer stated that "capital is measured in units of consumption goods."[5] Romer further described that capital is one of four inputs that are factored in production. The other three inputs are labor, human capital, and technology. Romer then modified the Cobb–Douglas production function to incorporate these four inputs in the equation.

Romer provides an interesting finding on the role of technology to create economic growth. A technological innovation can be controlled by one organization and yet can also be shared among other organizations. Romer explained how this is possible when an organization can claim ownership on a physical technological system, but it may not have ownership on the mere design or instructions of that physical product. Other organizations could gain access to the design, review it, make alterations, and design another physical form of the system. Those organizations with the technical skill to create a new technological system from the design would spur innovation further. The ideas in the design may not be owned, but the finished product that embodies the described ideas can be owned. While a physical technological system is tangible and complete, ideas are abstract and open to change. Thus, the design which is a formalization of ideas can be shared and changed. The further changes to the design made by others reflect the innovation through continuous improvement to the original design.

Back to the production function, Cobb–Douglas and Romer's modification serve a particular purpose to measure economic growth at the macroeconomic level. However, these equations are not appropriate to measure production at the individual organization level. Although both production functions can be used, the equations can be too unwieldy for analyzing operations on a daily basis. The mathematics involved is very sophisticated. A simpler production function that can be used in day-to-day operations would be preferred. And as discussed above, a business manager needs to analyze other types of resources in addition to labor. An appropriate equation must take into consideration all possible factors and should calculate each factor with a weight that has logical meaning. The use of an appropriate equation will allow the business manager to evaluate her operations in a way that leads to comparing the different factors and selecting the ones that will be best for her particular business.

1.3 Equipment and Labor: The Production Equation

Based on the foregoing discussion of operations and resources and a review of the Cobb–Douglas production function, I propose a new and straightforward production equation that would be easier to follow by many organizations across all industry sectors. This new equation can be adapted to suit the business of any organization. As explained below, some of the variables may be excluded if an organization deems them not applicable. All organizations should at the minimum factor in human labor, machine equipment, and all other costs (three variables). The production equation is defined as follows:

$$R \geq LC_l + EC_e + M_rC_r + M_pC_p + DC_d + C_a$$

where
R = Total revenue
L = Number of human workers (labor)
C_l = Unit cost (wage) of each human
E = Number of machine equipment
C_e = Unit cost of each machine
M_r = Number of raw materials
C_r = Unit cost of each raw material
M_p = Number of processed materials
C_p = Unit cost of each processed material
D = Amount of land used
C_d = Unit cost of each land used
C_a = Amount of all other costs

The production equation is a summation of five pairs of variables and the amount of all other costs. Each pair of variables is a product of an input quantity and its corresponding unit cost. The first pair multiplies the number of human workers by the unit cost of each human worker. The unit cost of a human worker is the wage or salary. The second pair multiplies the number of machine equipment by the unit cost of each machine. The third pair multiplies the number of raw materials by the unit cost of each raw material. The fourth pair multiplies the number of processed materials by the unit cost of each processed material. The last pair multiplies the amount of land used by the unit cost of each land used. The results of all five pairs and the amount of all other costs are finally summed up to arrive at the total production cost, which would be less than or equal to total revenue.

Total revenue is the product of the total number of goods or services produced or delivered and the unit price of each good or service. All the variables in the production equation contribute to producing the total number of goods or services.

Depending on industry sector and type of organization, the raw material, processed material, and land variables may not be applicable and may be excluded from the equation. If excluded, the respective input quantity and unit cost values are zero. Raw material refers to a natural resource, a mineral resource, or an unprocessed commodity in its natural state that an organization requires to produce a good or service. Processed material, on the other hand, includes supplies and manufactured materials that an organization requires to produce a good or service. Land includes the use of land that is required to produce a good or service. For example, an agricultural producer requires 10 acres of land to grow strawberries.

To ensure all possible costs are accounted for, all other items that cannot be classified under the five specific variables go into all other costs. This would include overhead. As this category is one large sum that covers many different items, input quantity is not applicable for all other costs.

This book and the examples described below apply a daily time period in the production equation. This means that the equation reflects how much production will cost to produce a good or service in one day, on average. An organization can change the time period to hourly, weekly, monthly, or yearly. If the time period is changed, the calculations of all variables must change to reflect the same time period.

Productivity equations can be derived from the production equation. Organizations can measure and compare output per input and cost per output at the individual resource level. For instance, labor cost per unit of output can be compared against machine cost per unit of output and raw material cost per unit of output. In another instance, output per unit of labor input can be compared against output per unit of machine input and output per unit of raw material input. This level of analysis would enable a business manager to find the optimal combination of resources to use.

The total cost per output productivity equation is defined as follows:

$$P_{co} = \frac{LC_l}{O} + \frac{EC_e}{O} + \frac{M_rC_r}{O} + \frac{M_pC_p}{O} + \frac{DC_d}{O} + \frac{C_a}{O}$$

where
P_{co} = Total cost per output productivity
O = Total output (total number of goods or services)
See the production equation for the meaning of all other variables.

The total cost per output productivity equation is a summation of all six individual cost per output resource productivity variables. Each variable can be used separately to compare it with other variables and the total cost per output productivity. With exception of all other costs, each variable is the product of the resource quantity and the resource cost divided by the total output. The cost per output for all other costs is the amount of all other costs divided by the total output. The raw material, processed material, and land variables may be excluded if their respective value of the input quantity is zero. Each individual cost per output metric indicates how much an input resource would cost to produce or deliver one good or service. The sum of the cost per output metrics provides an estimate of the overall cost of all inputs to produce or deliver one good or service.

The output per input productivity of an individual input resource is calculated using the following equation:

$$P_x = \frac{O}{X}$$

where
P_x = Output per input productivity of the input quantity X
O = Total output (total number of goods or services)
X = Replacement variable for L, E, M_r, M_p, or D (one of the five input quantity variables)

The results of P_x for all individual input resources are not summed up to a total value, because the total could be an erroneous value. The utility of this productivity metric is limited to comparing the individual input resources' output per input productivity against each other. Each input resource's output per input productivity is the quotient of the total output and the number of resources (human labor, machine equipment, etc.). The raw material, processed material, and land variables may be excluded if their respective value of the input quantity is zero. These three variables, if included however, may not provide anything meaningful for comparison. Inclusion of each variable can be determined on a case-by-case basis given the industry sector and type of organization. In general, human labor and machine equipment provide more meaning when analyzed both individually

Item Description	Input Quantity	Unit Cost	Total Cost	Cost per Output	Output per Input
Human Labor	30	$ 178.64	$ 5,359.20	$ 1.53	116.7
Machine Equipment	25	$ 100.00	$ 2,500.00	$ 0.71	140.0
Raw Material	100	$ 8.50	$ 850.00	$ 0.24	35.0
Processed Material	20	$ 15.25	$ 305.00	$ 0.09	175.0
Land	1	$ 65.75	$ 65.75	$ 0.02	3,500.0
All Other Costs		$ 2,000.00	$ 2,000.00	$ 0.57	
Total			**$ 11,079.95**	**$ 3.17**	
Item Description	Output Quantity	Unit Price	Total Revenue		
Product A	1,000	$ 12.25	$ 12,250.00		
Product B	500	$ 15.00	$ 7,500.00		
Product C	2,000	$ 7.50	$ 15,000.00		
Total	**3,500**		**$ 34,750.00**		
Net Revenue			**$ 23,670.05**		

Figure 1.1 Production cost and revenue worksheet for one operating scenario.

Source: Author's example of calculating production.

Note: The total cost per output may not add up exactly, due to rounding.

and together. The output per input productivity metric indicates how many goods or services would be produced or delivered per one input resource (one human worker or one machine).

Figure 1.1 provides a worksheet example of the resource and productivity calculations. Note that two tables are integrated to show the cost side in one table and the revenue side in another table. The two tables were combined for the purpose of displaying the content in an economical way in this book. On the revenue side, there may be one or more products or services. The sum total of all products or services is the total output. On the cost side, each resource item has a corresponding input quantity, unit cost, total cost, cost per output metric, and output per input metric. Input quantity and output per input are not applicable for all other costs. The net revenue calculation is the total cost of all resources subtracted from the total revenue of all products and services.

If any resource category has one or more subcategories with different unit costs, then the category needs to be broken down by subcategories. For example, there could be three groups of human workers, and each group can be paid a different wage. The worksheet then must be modified to list the quantity and cost of group 1, the quantity and cost of group 2, and the quantity and cost of group 3.

Any resource category with different units of quantity among its subcategories also needs to be broken down by subcategories. This is particularly true with raw and processed materials. One group of materials can be purchased in kilograms and another group can be purchased in liters. In this example, each group of materials must be listed separately: one for kilograms and the other for liters. Breaking up the resource categories into subcategories because of their different units of quantity and unit costs will produce a more accurate calculation of specific resources.

Most important, all calculations in the worksheet of Figure 1.1 represent the cost, revenue, and productivity for *one* operating scenario in a given time period. In the example, the combination of resources is for a typical day of business operation.

After the calculations have been completed, copy the total values, net revenue, cost per output value, and the output per input values for human labor and machine equipment to the table shown in Figure 1.2 and give the operating scenario a logical name. Figure 1.2 provides a worksheet to hold summaries of all possible operating scenarios. Another set of a combination of resources can be calculated in the table shown in Figure 1.1 to create a new operating scenario, and its summary values can be copied to the table shown in Figure 1.2. A business manager can then compare each operating scenario in relation to the other scenarios, analyzing which combination of resources in a particular scenario should be used. Each scenario's total cost, net revenue, and productivity metrics can be compared against those of other scenarios.

In Figure 1.2, "Mix Scenario 1" would be the best operating scenario to pursue, since this scenario has the lowest total production cost and could maximize profit. Productivity metrics indicate that Mix Scenario 1 has the lowest total cost per unit of output and could produce very high output among the share of 30 human workers and 25 machines. One machine could contribute to the production of 140 products, while one human could contribute to 116.7 products.

Item Description	Total Cost	Total Output	Total Revenue	Net Revenue	Cost per Output	Output per Human	Output per Machine
All Human	$ 21,084.75	3,500	$ 34,750.00	$ 13,665.25	$ 6.02	35.0	0.0
All Machine	$ 13,220.75	3,500	$ 34,750.00	$ 21,529.25	$ 3.78	0.0	35.0
Mix Scenario 1	$ 11,079.95	3,500	$ 34,750.00	$ 23,670.05	$ 3.17	116.7	140.0
Mix Scenario 2	$ 17,152.75	3,500	$ 34,750.00	$ 17,597.25	$ 4.90	70.0	70.0
Mix Scenario 3	$ 36,084.75	3,500	$ 34,750.00	$ (1,334.75)	$ 10.31	35.0	23.3

Figure 1.2   Total production cost and revenue for five operating scenarios.

Source: Author's example of showing production summaries of different operating scenarios, based on calculations done in the tables shown in Figure 1.1.

In contrast, "Mix Scenario 3" would be the worst operating scenario. With the highest total cost per unit of output metric at $10.31, the organization would have a loss exceeding $1,300. Even by implementing 150 machines (far more than would be needed), machine productivity would decrease.

Comparing the "All Human" and "All Machine" scenarios shows what one would expect in terms of cost. With the cost of machines lower than the cost of humans, there would be cost savings by around 37 percent. An interesting observation is that total cost and net revenue amounts are flipped in both scenarios. While either operating scenario could still be pursued, neither the All Human scenario nor the All Machine scenario would be the optimal choice.

The example operating scenarios demonstrate how to use the production equation. It is a good practice to generate a number of different scenarios to see how the organization's operation can be managed with a different combination of resources. The business manager would be able to identify which one may turn out either profitable or unprofitable. Who knows? Hidden among the various scenarios that can be imagined lurks the operating scenario that could be most advantageous to achieving business goals.

While the production equation is primarily for an individual organization to optimize its business, the production equation can also be used to calculate economic activity at the national or regional level. By disaggregating capital by machine equipment, raw material, processed material, and land, this formula could provide a complete and more accurate picture of the national economy. The data shown in Figure 1.2 could be changed to show the calculations of not the scenarios of one organization but the current year's financial situation of numerous organizations. The production equation as proposed and explained with its variables that describe business operations could be an alternative method to the Cobb–Douglas and Romer production functions.

1.4 An All-Human Labor Force

An "All-Human Labor Force" in theory is an operating scenario in which an organization completely depends on human workers to produce a good or service. In this scenario, the organization does not use any kind of machine equipment to produce the good or service. The organization operates with 100 percent humans and 0 percent machines. The All-Human Labor Force operates at one extreme end of the labor force spectrum.

1.5 An All-Machine Equipment Force

Operating at the other extreme end of the labor force spectrum is an "All-Machine Equipment Force." This operating scenario in theory is one in which an organization completely depends on machines designed to automate all aspects of its business. The organization has found ways to eliminate all human workers from handling all parts of the business. The organization operates with 0 percent humans and 100 percent machines.

1.6 A Mix Labor–Equipment Force

A "Mix Labor–Equipment Force" is in theory an operating scenario in which an organization has a combination of human labor and machine equipment to produce a good or service. Given the total number of resources, an organization may operate with 50 percent humans and 50 percent machines. Other organizations would have varying percentages, finding a balance in the mix. An organization may have 30 percent humans and 70 percent machines, for example. Another organization may have 60 percent humans and 40 percent machines. Along the labor force spectrum, organizations would start in the middle (the 50–50 percent scenario) and move out in either direction toward more humans or more machines to find an optimal mix. However they choose, organizations would move toward the All-Human Labor Force scenario or the All-Machine Equipment Force scenario.

The Mix Labor–Equipment Force, the All-Human Labor Force, and the All-Machine Equipment Force represent theoretical operating scenarios in which an organization could choose. These three scenarios serve more as reference points along the labor force spectrum to guide an organization on where it should operate. Based on an analysis of its resources, an organization could choose any point along the spectrum.

Notes

1 Charles W. Cobb and Paul H. Douglas (1928) "A Theory of Production," *The American Economic Review*, 18, no. 1, p. 151.
2 Cobb and Douglas, p. 165.
3 Robert M. Solow (1957) "Technical Change and the Aggregate Production Function," *The Review of Economics and Statistics*, 39, no. 3, p. 314.
4 Simon Baptist and Cameron Hepburn (2013) "Intermediate Inputs and Economic Productivity," *Philosophical Transactions of the Royal Society A*, 371, p. 18.
5 Paul M. Romer (1989) "Endogenous Technological Change," NBER Working Paper No. 3210, December 1989, *National Bureau of Economic Research*, p. 10.

Chapter 2

Technological Development

2.1 Chapter Summary

Chapter 2 explains the development of technologies, starting with the computer and moving on to how the computer and electronic parts have been integrated into machines and the human body. Recent research in electrical engineering, mechanical engineering, nanotechnology, and biology highlight advancements. The examples describe illustrative cases and are not exhaustive of all advancements. After describing the machines and devices, the chapter covers the evolution of data analysis, explaining how humans have calculated and analyzed data from ancient times to the modern era. The latest method in analyzing complex data types leads the business manager into understanding artificial intelligence (AI) in philosophical, technical, and business terms. With an idea on what it will take to implement an AI machine that can imitate a human, the chapter explains the quantum computer (a new type of computer) that will be a revolutionary advancement over the present-day microcomputer system. Based on the foregoing explanations, the chapter corrects misconceptions that the general public may have on emerging technologies. The chapter concludes with guiding points on how the business manager should assess whether parts of her business can be automated.

2.2 The Computer

A computer is a physical machine that comprises various parts connected in such a way as to process information into some useful form. A computer processor, a storage device, a memory module, a keyboard, and a display

DOI: 10.4324/9781003189329-3

monitor work together to a create a logical process to compute data.[1] From the outside, a person uses a keyboard to enter data into the computer. The configured parts inside the computer perform the computation on the entered data. Finally, the result of the computation is outputted for the person to see. This is the basic function of a computer.

A simple computer is a calculator. A person enters a mathematical formula, such as 10 plus 10 equals, for example. The electronic parts inside the calculator process the input. The output displays the answer, which is 20 in the example.

A complex computer is a personal computer typically used in an office or a home. A person types letters, numbers, and other characters on the keyboard. She sees the results immediately on a display monitor. The electronic parts inside the personal computer are processing the characters. The person enters a command to save the information. The electronic parts take the command to store the displayed information in a particular format.

A more advanced computer configuration can eliminate the need for a person to enter data. Another computer sends letters, numbers, and other characters in one long uninterrupted stream. The two computers are connected, which may be in the same office building or in different countries, to send and receive the data without human involvement. The internal parts in the first computer push out the data to the second computer, where the internal parts of the second computer process the incoming data. The second computer may save the processed data in its storage device. The second computer may also output the result in another long uninterrupted stream back to the first computer, where the internal parts of the first computer will process the new data. This configuration of two computers creates a simple form of automation in which data are processed in the computers without involvement of a person.

Additional parts may be connected to the computer. But the additional parts would not fundamentally change the basic logical process of computing data. The second computer in the just mentioned example replaces a person to input data. Various types of other parts that can be connected would add value to the operation of the computer. An example is a computer network adapter that allows the computer to communicate with another computer. Other parts or elements could be a computer network, the Internet, embedded technology, or emerging technology. Such elements that are components in the information technology (IT) ecosystem build upon the operation of a computer to create additional functions that extend the purpose and usefulness of the computer.[2] As it will be described below, other types of components can be added to make the computer more useful.

2.3 The Computer and the Internet

A computer can be connected to the Internet, which is one large global computer network where multiple computers can exchange information using standardized protocols. For example, a computer located in the United States can send and receive data to and from a computer located in India. The particular computer may be a smartphone, a personal computer, or another form that contains the basic parts to operate the logical process of computing. Regardless of the particular form of the computer, all of the computers communicate on the Internet through a standard protocol such as HTTP, HTTPS, or SMTP. The Internet protocol provides the mechanism by which the Internet can be connected to the computer.

The connected computers use a computer software program to handle text, images, video, and other types of information. The software program follows an Internet standard in order for the computers to process and display the specific type of information. The World Wide Web (WWW), which is the most widely used application of the Internet, has a specialized software program that operates in each computer wherein the software processes the data. A Web browser software program, which is typically used by people, displays information to a person. The person can use the Web browser to enter data and send it to another computer. The receiving computer has a Web software program developed in such a way as to accept the person's data for processing. Another kind of software program can perform complicated functions other than simply displaying and entering data on a person's computer. This kind of software still follows an Internet/Web standard in order for the data to be accepted and processed by the receiving computer.

Other applications of the Internet such as sending and receiving messages, transmitting electronic files, and streaming video productions would have a specialized computer software program to handle such particular type of information. In order to be processed by a computer on the Internet, however, those software programs still must follow an Internet standard.

Since the mid-1990s, the world has seen rapid growth of various kinds of computer software programs to process information on the Internet. Electronic mail (e-mail) was the first kind of software that found wide acceptance by computer users. Publishing information on a Web site was the next software program that quickly grew in popularity. The relative ease of creating a Web site allowed the number of personal and commercial Web sites to proliferate around the world. As infrastructure improved to transmit data faster and more reliably and as more people came online in increasing numbers, entrepreneurs saw opportunities to develop Web software programs to serve people in numerous ways. It started with being able to search information from all available Web sites. It accelerated with being able to purchase goods and services through an electronic commerce (e-commerce) software program. It moved into the corporate environment where companies and partners can efficiently share business information through an Intranet or Extranet software program.

Further changes to the computer hardware made it possible for a person to access information from a location that was not tied by a wire. Up until the turn of the 21st century, people were limited to using Internet applications from a personal computer that had to be connected by an Ethernet cable. Wireless devices were developed to connect to the computer network without an Ethernet cable. Computer advancements in the last 10 years created smaller electronic parts that added the logical process of computing inside a cellular phone. The integration of computer functions converted the cellular phone into a smartphone – that is, a handheld device that can be used as a phone and a computer.

The cellular network, of course, would have to change to accommodate both voice and data. From the late 1990s, telecommunication providers re-engineered their transmission towers and network equipment to allow data to be carried across their network. New Internet protocols were designed and eventually established as a standard. The improvement in the wireless network coupled with a handheld computer device allowed a person to connect to the Internet and use an Internet application from any location not bound by a wired network.

2.4 The Computer and Mechanical Devices

As it has been shown with the phone, advancements in electronic parts as being smaller and just as powerful as in a personal computer can convert other devices into computers. The possibility could open the door for a wide range of mechanical equipment to be computerized.

The integration of mechanical engineering and electronics is not new however. Tetsuro Mori, who worked at the Yaskawa Electric Corporation in Japan, had coined the term "Mechatronics" in 1969 by combining the words mechanical and electronic to describe a new type of electronic control system.[3] Such a system incorporates electronic devices and circuits to create controls that would regulate the behavior and movement of the mechanical apparatus comprising gears, shafts, and motors. Mechatronics, however, did not gain popularity until the late 1980s, when it was widely adopted in the European Union.[4] It is now globally accepted as improving the efficiency and effectiveness of machines in the manufacturing industry. Engineers eventually realized how much of the mechanical functions in machinery could be controlled by electronic circuits.

A critical component that controls the movement of certain parts in a machine is a servo motor (servo). A servo motor is more complicated than a motor. Whereas a motor outputs rotational energy (e.g., spins a turbine), a servo motor converts rotational energy into linear motion through its connection to gears and a shaft. An electronic circuit is a part of the servo motor to decrease the speed of the motor so as to move the shaft with greater precision. A motor itself usually runs continuously at a constant speed, but a servo motor can change its speed as needed to meet certain output objectives.

Earlier servo motors in the 1970s and 1980s were limited in application. The servo motor used direct current powered by a battery. The servo and its parts were quite small and made of plastic. A complete servo would fit in the palm of a hand. These earlier servos created a community of hobbyists who built and played with radio-controlled model airplanes. A servo in a model airplane pushed and pulled rods to control the ailerons on the plane's wing. A person on the ground used a handheld device to send the input of whether the ailerons were to move up or down through a radio frequency sent to the electronic circuit in the airplane.

Servo motors improved over the years, becoming larger and heavier to support manufacturing applications. The larger servos, using alternating current, meant it could push or turn steel parts in a machine. Two applications showed the power of a servo motor to move a 2,000-pound printing wheel in a printing press and to position logs precisely in a sawmill.[5]

A particular application that has demonstrated high utility of servo motors is robotics. Because of its precision to control movement that can be repeated a number of times in predictable ways, a servo motor can be built into joints to move arms with dexterity.[6] Along an assembly line, a robotic arm fitted with a servo could pick up a small part from the conveyor belt at the exact moment, raise it up 12 inches, rotate 90 degrees, drop the part in a bin, and finally return to its original position to pick up another part. In another example, an automated welding machine equipped with a robotic arm and a servo motor could solder steel parts quickly and accurately with little to no faults.

An electronic part that can be integrated into a machine is a sensor, which is a device that converts a physical property into an electrical signal. Such a device can perform like a switch to control how the electronic circuit operates. Instead of having a physical switch where a person has to turn the circuit on or off, a sensor is connected to detect automatically any change to an external property that it is designed to capture. A light sensor, for instance, captures the presence and amount of light and converts that energy into an electronic input to tell another component in the circuit what to do. The change from darkness to light could tell the circuit to sound an alarm, for example. A solar panel uses photovoltaic cells, which are light sensors, to convert sunlight into voltage. The sensor uses specialized sensitive material to detect the physical property of sunlight.

A wide range of sensors have been developed. A type of image sensor creates an image by processing the amount of light through numerous pixels that which in turn convert the light into electrical charges. The quality of the image is dependent on the format and resolution of the image sensor and other factors. A type of temperature sensor detects the amount of heat and converts the change in heat to reduce or increase the amount of resistance in the electronic circuit. A type of pressure sensor converts the amount of pressure applied to a diaphragm into a proportional amount of voltage. An accelerometer is a type of sensor that detects vibration or motion in an object and converts that kind of energy into an electrical signal. Other types of sensors include the ability to detect and measure whether an object has moved, the relative distance of an object to another object, the position of a valve or gate, the amount and rate of a flow of liquid, and the level of a gas or chemical.

An emerging type of sensor can detect the biological, chemical, or physical process in the human body. Various types of health- and medical-related sensors are being experimented to carry out different functions such as to monitor patient health and record brain activity.[7] These sensors may be placed directly on the skin or implanted surgically inside the body.

Any type of sensor can be active or passive. An active sensor is a sensor that requires an external power source to operate. A passive sensor does not need an external power source and can be powered by the energy that it detects. A medical-related sensor that is implanted in the human body would be a passive sensor.

A mechanical machine could be transformed into a computerized machine by incorporating a sensor, a servo motor, and a computer into the design of the machine. The logical process of computing would take an input from the sensor and execute the input as a command. The command would be sent to the servo to change the speed, direction, or movement of a connected arm to do some particular work. Another sensor attached to the end of the arm would return input, a certain amount of pressure for example. The servo might be programmed to change the movement again in an adjustment that is proportional to the amount of detected pressure. This simplified example illustrates how the new machine can automatically do work and react to a certain change. The example, moreover, could operate without human involvement.

2.5 The Computer and New Materials

Integrating new machines with the computer would require new materials. Steel, aluminum, and other metals would continue to work in heavy machinery. But they may not be appropriate or optimal in machines designed for health and non-manufacturing industries. The physical case that encloses the entire system would have to be so tiny that the use of conventional materials could cause problems or create design issues. A power supply would also have to change. The electronic components too would have to change in form and substance.

For decades, silicon has been the main material to develop the processing power of a computer. Manufacturers of computer processors have been able to increase the number of transistors exponentially in a smaller unit of space. But silicon has its limits in how many transistors can be packed in an infinitesimally small processor. A processor with billions of transistors generates considerable heat, and a phenomenon occurs when electrons free themselves to leave holes that silicon cannot manage very well.[8] This results in serious speed and performance degradation.

Adding germanium to silicon is one way to manage the phenomenon of holes created by freed electrons. One manufacturer claimed to have boosted performance of current processors by as much as four times with the development of silicon-germanium processors.[9]

Other materials that have been used and could replace silicon are gallium arsenide and gallium nitride.

Coming out of the field of nanotechnology is a material that could be used in a wide range of applications across multiple industry sectors. Scientists in this field manipulate atoms to create new forms at the molecular level. Graphene is a material that is formed by a single layer of carbon atoms in a hexagonal lattice structure. The thickness of the layer is about 0.335 nanometers or one atom. Being the thinnest material, graphene can bend and change its shape without breaking. A sheet of graphene can be rolled into a tube to create a carbon nanotube.

Compared to silicon, a carbon atom is 30 percent smaller and weighs 57 percent lighter than a silicon atom. With a melting point that is 1.6 times higher than silicon, carbon can withstand stress at an extremely high temperature. While both silicon and carbon have the same number of valence electrons, silicon uses all four electrons to bond with other silicon atoms. This requires an amount of energy to break an electron free that will create electrical conduction. Carbon in the form of graphene, on the other hand, uses three of its valence electrons to bond with other carbon atoms in the graphene structure.[10] The fourth valence electron in the graphene's carbon atom is naturally free, allowing it to create electrical conduction.

The band gap, which determines how much a material can conduct electricity, creates an unusual conical shape that leaves no separation between the valence band and the conduction band. In this regard, graphene acts like a metal. Some distance is necessary between the valence and conduction bands in order to control and manage the flow of electrons.[11]

Making graphene and carbon nanotubes to act less like a metal and more like a semiconductor has been a major challenge. Researchers and engineers at Stanford University developed a method to control the conductive properties in nanotubes to design the first computer built from nanotubes.[12] The result produced a computer with 178 transistors made of nanotubes. Work continued on the manufacturing process to develop semiconducting carbon nanotubes. And scientists announced in 2019 the development of a 16-bit computer processor that used 14,000 transistors made of nanotubes.[13] The manufacturing process involved a chemical solution to separate metallic carbon nanotubes from semiconducting ones, adding a polymer and organizing the semiconducting carbon nanotubes on a substrate.

Organic chemistry has been involved to develop organic transistors. Pentacene, oliogothiophenes, hexadecafluorocopper, phthalocyanine, and polythiophene are sublimed and solution-processed semiconductors that are being explored. Progress has resulted in producing an electronic circuit made with 864 organic field-effect transistors (OFETs) in a 48-stage shift register circuit.[14] An early application of an OFET is in development of a thin and bendable active-matrix display screen.

An advantage of organic transistors is that the material can be sensitive to touch. A new area of application is to create organic transistors that can respond to pressure, temperature, and stimuli. Researchers explored the development of a sensor that uses a low-voltage OFET that responds to force and temperature.[15] Researchers on another project blended a semiconducting polymer and an insulating elastomer to create a stretchable and self-healing semiconductor film that behaves like human skin.[16] The material is built with an active-matrix array of sensors and organic transistors. Researchers tested the self-healing semiconductor film with a low voltage that would be safe to use in a medical device.

Conventional electronics continue to be made with metals, inorganic chemicals, and other materials that can be harmful to the environment. This creates a dilemma on how to dispose of old computers and electronic devices that can no longer be used. To address the problem of electronic waste, researchers designed a novel approach to develop a semiconducting polymer on an extremely thin (800 nanometers) substrate made of biodegradable cellulose.[17] Researchers found that the material can completely disintegrate in a mild acidic solution after 30 days.

Using less hazardous chemicals is being experimented with to develop new types of batteries that can better hold an electrical charge and can be safer overall. In 2004, Sony announced a new silver-oxide battery that no longer uses mercury.[18] Previously, mercury was used to suppress the corrosive effect of zinc. Sony used a higher quality zinc alloy manufactured into a powder that can reduce corrosion. Researchers experimented with triallyl phosphate to improve the stability of a lithium-ion battery at high voltage and high temperature conditions.[19] Scientists found a new way to charge a battery by stacking two layers of sodium atoms between layers of graphene.[20] The scientists simulated the experiment with lithium atoms and showed that stacked lithium in increasing layers reduced stability more than the increased layers of stacked sodium. Other researchers experimented with ion-charged sodium, potassium, zinc, and aluminum, and the results looked promising to replace the lithium-ion battery with those materials.[21]

Currently, lithium-ion batteries are widely used in computers, digital cameras, and smartphones. A hazard for using the lithium-ion battery, however, is that it can get warm quickly and could potentially catch on fire.

2.6 The Computer and the Human Body

Safer batteries, organic transistors, miniaturized sensors, and other advancements could make their way into developing computer-based medical devices. A significant challenge, however, remains in the device's design that can supply electrical power and transmit an electronic signal with a minimum requirement to maintain the device's functionality. The quality of the electronic parts and battery inside a computerized device can degrade over time through extensive use and normal wear and tear. Once implanted in the body, a device that malfunctions or becomes inoperable will have to be repaired or replaced. An ideal computerized medical device would be one that can be self-powered, self-healing, and well-integrated into the human body.

Intrabody communication provides a method of transmitting electronic signals through the body by using the conductive properties of human tissue.[22] Skin, muscle, and organ tissue could be used like a wire to send a signal. Two physical probes attached to areas of the body would communicate with each other by sending and receiving signals through the skin. Two electrodes can be implanted in muscle or the brain and use that muscle or brain to transmit and receive signals.

Researchers developed a device that combines near field communication (NFC) technology and temperature and pressure sensors to monitor the health of a patient.[23] This device does not require a battery and instead gets its power through the interaction of the NFC tag and a reader. NFC operates on a radio frequency to transmit and receive a signal wirelessly within a few centimeters. In an experiment, 65 of these ultrathin sensor devices, each one of which just larger than a penny, were spread across the human body and tested to capture the body's physiological changes over time. A smartphone installed with a computer software program captured and displayed the data of each sensor device.

A complete system comprised of a computer processor, a display screen, a zinc-manganese dioxide battery, photovoltaic cells, and a glucose sensor was designed to be worn like a wristwatch to monitor glucose level through a person's sweat.[24] This type of wearable technology gets its power from light and converts and stores the light energy in the rechargeable battery.

Another way of monitoring the health of a patient is by a pill-sized device that can be swallowed.[25] A research team tested a device with an electret microphone in pigs to monitor heart and respiratory rates. The small non-invasive device recorded data as it traveled through the pig's body from mouth to rectum. The team conducted experiments to test how well the device reacts to the environmental conditions that normally occur inside the gastrointestinal tract.

The work in DNA[26] sequencing shows that a motor and a computer processor can be made from DNA, which is a hereditary material found in humans and other living organisms. Such a design could create a molecular machine that converts chemical energy in the body into motion. Unlike devices described above that require metals, semiconductors, plastic, and other materials foreign to the human body, DNA could potentially be used as the raw material to produce a machine that would likely not have damaging side effects when used inside the body.

DNA strands were manipulated to create an object that mimics walking.[27] The object would draw energy from the DNA and convert it into motion.

The CRISPR/Cas9 technology was used to develop a computer processor programmed in a single cell.[28] Researchers demonstrated that this type of processor could perform computations.

2.7 Computing Methods of Data Analysis

The driving force behind the development of the technologies described above would be the need to collect and use data with greater speed, precision, and efficiency. What has been described thus far are machines and devices – mere tools to do some kind of work. And so, the discussion turns to data itself and the evolution of how humans have been able to calculate and analyze data.

What is data or datum in singular form? Data are facts that can be measured and used for planning and reasoning.[29] The singular form, datum, refers to a single fact that can be measured.

For millennia, humans have needed to measure facts. In ancient times dating back as early as 2400 BCE, the Babylonians, ancient Egyptians, Greeks, Romans, Indians, Chinese, Koreans, and Japanese created a form of an abacus to count numbers.[30] Among its many forms, the abacus was a tool that allowed a person to move beads or pebbles along a rod or a groove. While the person relied on using his brain to do the addition and subtraction, the abacus provided a way to record the calculation so that he could not forget it. He could then show his calculated result in the abacus to his friend. The abacus was a manual type of calculator in which the limiting factor was on the speed of the person's brain.

Although the abacus can still be found in use in Asian countries today, the tools of calculation have advanced over the last 60 years. A slide rule was a simple yet ingenious way of finding the answer to complicated mathematics problems involving logarithms, square roots, and trigonometry functions. A person moved a stiff material made of thick card stock or wood to align a numbered scale with the scale displayed on the unmovable part of the slide rule. It was like a ruler. The alignment of the two numbered scales resulted in a calculated number. The slide rule made it faster to find the answer. The alternative method was to write the mathematical formula in a number of steps by hand on paper.

With new computer processors that made for the emergence of the personal computer in the 1970s, an electronic device was developed to do addition, subtraction, multiplication, and division. This modern-day calculator equipped with a processor, a display screen, and a numbered keypad replaced the slide rule. Instead of moving a scale, a person can press numbers and a mathematical function and let the computer processor to do the calculation automatically. Newer versions of the electronic calculator would be developed to allow the person to calculate logarithms and trigonometry functions and show the result in a chart. The example of the calculator illustrates the ease with which a single person can compute numbers.

A computer more sophisticated than a calculator such as a mainframe, a computer server, and a supercomputer showed the capability to compute larger amounts of numbers at a higher volume and a faster rate – especially when accessible by several people. A team of mathematicians, statisticians, and researchers would use such a computer to work productively to calculate increasingly complex mathematical formulas. Beyond basic math and trigonometry, averages, proportions, hypothesis testing, linear regression, and other statistical measures would be programmed in the computer. The computer would then execute the advanced statistical measure and generate a more interesting output that allows a researcher to draw a logical conclusion. The computer, in effect, aids the researcher in processing large data sets.

John Tukey, a renowned statistician, came to the realization the role that statistics played in data analysis. In a 1962 article, he explained how mathematical statistics was not the central focus of but was a part of data analysis. Tukey explained that data analysis functions as a science with all the requirements that go into a scientific discipline. Statistics, on the other hand, is not really a science. Statistics provides methods and techniques derived from mathematics. In that sense, statistics is like a tool. Tukey posited that "data analysis must use mathematical argument and mathematical results as bases for judgment rather than as bases for proof or stamps of validity."[31] Tukey further stated and warned that the work of analyzing data can result in answers that may not be 100 percent certain and very likely may be wrong. Through the rigor of scientific inquiry, the process of data analysis would examine all the answers – right and wrong, certain and uncertain – and identify those answers that reasonably fit the research question.

Tukey's proposition of data analysis as a science and the role of statistics would not be revisited until half a century later. The latest advancements in computer technologies that have made it possible to compute a massive amount of data, which John Tukey could have dreamt of, have spawned a new field called data science. The introduction of this new field has caused a stir and some angst among contemporary statisticians. Applied statisticians and professional statistics organizations questioned the new term and asked have not they been doing data science all along.[32] The new field actually enlarges the scope of activities traditionally covered in university statistics departments and creates structure to ensure that the methods, processes, and technologies involved in data analysis can be carried out in a scientific manner. Tukey described such an environment best with the analogy of a laboratory where numerous trial runs on the data would be examined, and each subsequent experiment would get closer to a result that approximately matches the truth.

A certain type of data arguably may have influenced the creation of the new data science field. Up to this point, the discussion has focused on calculating numbers. But data can come in different types. A specific datum can be a string of text characters, a document, a photograph, an audio file, a video file, or a combination of all types. Considering these other types of data, how can a statistician input such non-quantifiable data for processing and analysis?

Advancements in computer technologies have led to improvements in saving and processing documents, images, and other complex file types. Block-level storage, for instance, provides greater reliability and increased efficiency in retrieving complex file types, which are stored in blocks as opposed to the conventional method of storing files in a file system. NoSQL allows a database to change to new data requirements that may not be known at the start of a project by eliminating the requirement of establishing relationships between data in several tables and instead creating key-value pairs on individual data elements. This is in contrast to a traditional relational database where all possible data elements need to be known beforehand. Server virtualization increases the speed and reduces the cost of provisioning new computer servers as needed by creating numerous software-based servers in a single physical computer server. Each of these software servers programmed to run a database or to process data can be created in seconds or minutes as opposed to a few hours for a traditional server. These example innovations highlight how engineers have solved technical problems to handle different data types and to serve and process data faster and reliably at larger scale.

Technology aside, new methods and procedures have had to be developed to analyze data types that are not quantifiable. Probabilistic method is a technique that draws on probability theory. A computer that uses the probabilistic method evaluates a random variable against a set of defined conditions and gives a probability value to the random variable based on how well it matches the conditions. Another method draws on how neurons operate in the human brain. An artificial neural network (also known as a neural net) comprises nodes distinguished by input nodes, hidden nodes, and output nodes. Each node would hold a specific datum. A computer processes the nodes to find connections and the strengths of those connections among the various nodes. Machine learning, which can be divided into three areas (supervised learning, unsupervised learning, and reinforcement learning), provides a method for a computer to analyze different types of data to find a specific match or a pattern. Machine learning requires a massive amount of data, which the computer can base its conclusions on.

All of these methods have an algorithm that is much more than a mathematical formula. An equation may be the central part, but there would be one or more rules that direct what will be the output. The rules forming part of the algorithm would be based on logic and reasoning. As the computer processes the complex data types, the computer would be processing through a number of rules until a match or a close approximation can be found.

Here is where the output of an analysis of complex data types can be fraught with issues. Who is defining the rules to construct an algorithm to determine, for example, what should be an action in response to seeing an image that shows a person holding up a finger or two fingers? The engineer will have an educational level, a certain amount of knowledge, a particular background, and extensive or limited experience that would influence how a rule is defined. He may interpret the behavior in the image as an attack and write a rule to take some kind of retaliatory action. The computer then will take the rule and determine that the image is portraying hostile behavior when in reality that may not be the case. The rule and the algorithm as a whole as defined by the engineer's particular thinking can be shown to be faulty. In the provided example, the portrayal of the behavior could have a positive, negative, or neutral meaning depending on the culture and context of the image. Based on the culture in which the engineer was raised, he would be making an unintentional and potentially grave error in judgment.

2.8 Artificial Intelligence (AI)

The previous section on how data analysis has evolved would suggest that the computer is beginning to think like a human. Alan Turing wrote about such a possibility in a 1950 article in the journal *Mind*. He proposed a test (widely hailed as the "Turing Test") to determine whether a computer can convince a third-party person that it is the real human in a question-and-answer session with an actual person. The computer and the live person would engage in a conversation, and the third-party person must decide which one is really a human. The third-party person cannot see the participants but can only hear ideally read the participants' responses in written form. The Turing Test is a demonstration of how well a computer can imitate a human. Alan Turing estimated that it would not be until 2000 (50 years from publishing the article) that a computer with sufficient storage capacity will be able to pass his test.[33]

If the objective is to build a computer that can think like a human, then the computer would need to have a brain like a human. The brain is the closest analogy to a computer processor. An adult male human brain can have about 86 billion neurons,[34] each one of which having a capacity to hold information. Sensory, motor, and other types of neurons carry messages to and from the brain, by way of electrical impulses and chemical signals, to control the functioning of organs, muscles, and the nervous system.[35] The computer processor performing like a human brain would need to have the capacity to process 86 billion nodes of data and send the information to various parts of the computer. And the processor would have to do it in a fraction of a second.

Based on Turing's estimation, the construction of a computer capable of imitating a human has not been completed yet. Widely publicized successes such as IBM Watson's win against a challenger at the television gameshow "Jeopardy!" and the defeat of a Go player by Google's AlphaGo showed a high level of a computer's intelligence. But these notable achievements are not exemplars of true AI. IBM and Google had programmed their machines for a specific purpose. Those same machines would have to be reprogrammed to learn and carry out another subject just as complicated as "Jeopardy!" or Go.

René Descartes, a French philosopher, contemplated what a machine would look like if it were to behave like a human. He came to the conclusion that the machine's behavior would necessarily have to be so diverse as to be able to react to any and all kinds of situations that life throws at the machine – an impossible feat for a machine, concluded Descartes.[36] Another way of saying this is what Alan Turing would call the absence of random behavior.[37] A computer after all is designed to do computations in a straightforward manner that follow logical courses of action. A computer behaves perfectly rational – and without emotion. A human, on the other hand, does not always behave rationally. Depending on the circumstance, the given situation, or personal mood, a person can change her mind on a whim with no apparent reason. A person's ability to reason however fallible it may be is not present in a computer.

Alan Turing suggested that the computer should be programmed with a random element.[38] Such a feature would allow the computer to find an alternate, more efficient approach to solving a problem – especially a complicated one that has thousands of variables to compute. Without a random element, the computer would have to follow a standard procedure in one long activity. And if it has to carry out the procedure several times, the computer would have to execute each procedure every time from beginning to end. Randomness could start somewhere in the middle of the procedure, allowing the length of time of the procedure's execution to be shortened. The development of some kind of randomness in the procedure could enable the computer to try something new at an instant and learn from it. It might be possible to program random behavior in a way that mimics the fallibility of human reasoning.

Replicating cognition in the computer is a daunting task but not an impossibility. However AI is developed, passing the Turing Test can be achieved eventually. A strategy is to develop AI in stages akin to the growth of a person from infant to adult. Current AI machines can be considered like children. Children explore their surroundings and learn what they need to know in order to survive. In this sense, an AI machine is collecting as much data as it can and learning what the data mean. Machine learning is designed to train a computer to learn all the inputted data. Over time, the AI machine would develop a rich repository of knowledge from which it can draw upon to take certain actions. At a certain point, the AI machine would have a level of maturity that matches an adult.

Another approach is to define the concept of AI in concrete terms. Davenport explains three types of AI that make sense in business applications. He divides AI into (1) robotic process automation (RPA), (2) cognitive insight, and (3) cognitive engagement.[39] The robots in RPA are not intelligent agents but are pre-defined scripts written to carry out mundane (often repetitive) tasks. Many such tasks relate to office administration and financial accounting. RPA involves automating a part of an organization's business process. Davenport describes RPA as "the least expensive and easiest to implement" over the other two types.[40] RPA will not pass the Turing Test.

Cognitive insight uses machine learning to provide much deeper analysis of an organization's data than what has been done in the past. This type of AI is more expensive since it requires sufficient computing resources to handle a massive amount of data. But the benefits include creating accurate models and forecasts and understanding the behaviors and interests of customers in more precise ways. The level of cognition is limited in the number and variety of rules that are programmed in the computer. An algorithm in this category would be specific to a particular business domain. An algorithm developed for one business domain may not be useful in another business domain. It is unlikely that cognitive insight can pass the Turing Test.

The third type of AI that Davenport explains is cognitive engagement. This type of AI uses machine learning and natural language processing to create an intelligent agent that can interact with a live person. Cognitive engagement would embody a robot who answers the questions asked by a human and offers recommendations. So constructed with a random element as described above could make this robot effective in conversing with a human. In many cases, customers turn to a customer service representative when they feel frustrated after trying to solve a problem on their own. The intelligent agent in this case might be programmed to recognize the customer's frustration and sort of have empathy with the customer. Cognitive engagement, if it is well designed and mature enough, can pass the Turing Test. Unfortunately, as Davenport cites with an illustrative example, cognitive engagement remains an immature type of AI.

The foregoing three types of AI remotely resemble the stages of reaching full maturity of an artificially intelligent machine. RPA is at the lowest level where an AI machine is capable of doing elementary tasks. Cognitive insight is at an intermediate level where an AI machine is capable of generating interesting and relevant findings. Cognitive engagement is at a high level where an AI machine is capable of interacting with a human.

2.9 Quantum Computer

The theory of quantum mechanics in physics holds promise in a new type of computer that would replace the present-day microcomputer system. The quantum computer would be the perfect choice to build an AI machine that can pass the Turing Test.

The quantum computer is fundamentally different, operating at the molecular level. It uses electrons or photons called quantum bits or qubits to hold data. Unlike in a present-day computer where one bit can be either 1 or 0, a single qubit can be both 1 and 0 at the same time. This is known as superposition where the state of 1 and the state of 0 are combined. Having the capacity to hold two states simultaneously allows the quantum computer to do two calculations per qubit at once. Two qubits (i.e., the atomic particles either electrons or photons) can interact with each other in what is called entanglement and share the same state.[41] In this pair of qubits, "changing the state of one [qubit] will instantaneously change the state of the other [qubit] in a predictable way."[42] Adding one more qubit in the process of entanglement can in theory increase the number of calculations exponentially (two qubits can do four calculations, three qubits can do eight calculations, four qubits can do 16 calculations, and so on).

For a quantum computer to surpass the computing power of a present-day computer, hundreds or thousands of qubits would need to be entangled. Current quantum computers in operation as of 2021 have 50 to 128 qubits.

The main challenge to developing a quantum computer is in how to control the atomic particles. The operation of a quantum computer has to be kept cold at an extremely low temperature or maintained in a vacuum chamber. Any slight vibration or change can cause the qubits to lose their superposition.[43] And the loss of superposition would mean the loss of data. Allowing oxygen to enter the interior of the quantum computer can cause magnetic noise (i.e., errors).[44] By the nature of how atomic particles behave, the quantum computer is extremely sensitive.

Other challenges include saving data in some form of quantum memory and transmitting data across some form of a quantum network. Researchers are working on quantum memory and quantum networks to make the quantum computer practical in use. These other components would create a complete quantum computing system.

Established companies such as IBM and Google and emerging start-up enterprises have quantum computers available to use. But they would be available as a remote service to which a present-day computer can connect via the Internet. Because of the challenge of controlling the particles, current quantum computers cannot be mass produced in a form that can be used in an individual business or home. Akin to the mainframe era where terminals were connected to a centralized mainframe, present-day computers would connect to a centralized quantum computer located in a remote location.

2.10 Misconceptions of Emerging Technologies

After reviewing the literature and analyzing how the latest advancements work, I clarify on some misconceptions that the general public may have regarding the quantum computer, AI, machine learning, robotics, and big data. The following five statements are the corrections to the misconceptions.

2.10.1 *Misconception 1 and Its Corrected Statement: Big Data Refers to the Inclusion of New Data Types that Hitherto Have Never Been Processed*

Computers have always been able to process large data sets in the past. But those types of records were in the form of numbers and text. Text in this case was limited to a few words. Text would have been converted into a numeric code wherever possible. Earlier software programs had limitations on the format and length in which data can be stored. Advancements in computer technologies have made it possible to process documents, images, and rich media files such as audio and video. And the Internet has made it possible to access all of these electronic files. Big data then is having the capability to access a wide range of data types beyond numbers and simple text and to process them in some effective and economical way.

2.10.2 *Misconception 2 and Its Corrected Statement: Robots Will Likely Be Precision Machines that Can Carry Out Defined and Specific Tasks*

The field of robotics is an area where the computer and electronic parts can be designed to control the movements and properties of the mechanical parts in a machine with dexterity and accuracy. With further advancements in new materials, these electronic-mechanical machines can be made smaller and power efficient – small enough to be implanted in the human body for health care purposes. The potential for making robots anything more that could pose an existential threat to humanity is highly speculative and driven more so by science fiction. A human-like robot that could overpower a human will need to have a high level of intelligence that matches that of a human.

2.10.3 Misconception 3 and Its Corrected Statement: Machine Learning Provides a New Method to Build the Capacity of the Computer to Analyze a Massive Amount of Data

The computer needs instructions and rules on how it can analyze the wide range of data types. Like a child in the process of learning a new subject, the computer has to learn about a new subject. The data set provides training data to learn from. A human engineer would supervise the computer to check that it is making logical connections. A system of rewards and punishments would be designed to teach the computer how to correct itself when it has made a wrong analysis and to remember not to make the wrong analysis again. Machine learning is more of a method to teach the computer on sifting through all the available data to find matches and patterns.

2.10.4 Misconception 4 and Its Corrected Statement: Artificial Intelligence Can Be Best Described as Varied Levels of Intelligence that a Computer Can Demonstrate

The level of AI described by Turing and Descartes is the ultimate level. Current computers are not there yet, however. Another form of AI is what machine learning is working to show. In this form, the computer demonstrates its capability to process and analyze data better than what a human can do. A human can only analyze a certain amount of data in a given time period. Whether the result of the analysis is certain or reliable, that will be up to the human to decide. A computer that is capable of making a correct decision more than 75 percent of the time would reflect another level of AI. Seen in this way, AI can be implemented across a continuum scale from elementary child-like intelligence to fully matured adult intelligence.

2.10.5 Misconception 5 and Its Corrected Statement: The Quantum Computer Will Operate Alongside the Present-Day Microcomputer System, Carrying out Computing Tasks that Today's Computers Cannot Do Efficiently

The future is still several decades if not a century away from seeing quantum computers replace present-day microcomputer systems. The physical operating challenge, the significant number of qubits necessary to do computations, the method of storing data, and the method of transferring data will all have to be resolved. In the meantime, it is likely that quantum computers will be developed for certain tasks such as factorization of numbers and optimization of computing processes. The quantum computer will have a role that augments computing resources and computing power with that of present-day computers.

2.11 Candidates for Business Automation

Here are some guiding points for assessing whether or not parts of the business should be automated. As the business manager reads the next several chapters, he should keep in mind these guiding points.

2.11.1 Definite Candidates for Business Automation

The following jobs are definite candidates for business automation. The cost of implementation would be relatively inexpensive. The risk to disrupting business operations would be low.

- Jobs that are very specific that lead to a definite end result.
- Jobs that are repeated following the same sequence of steps that end with the same predictable result.
- Jobs that are designed to retrieve stored information and send it to output with no analysis (i.e., there is no transformation to the data).

2.11.2 Possible Candidates for Business Automation

The following jobs may be candidates for business automation. It would depend on how much risk the organization is willing to bear in losing some control in the business process. It would also depend on how much the organization has to spend on computer technologies.

- Jobs that have low- to medium-stakes decision-making, which will have low to moderate consequence on business operations.
- Jobs that undergo a substantial change or some kind of transformation prior to being outputted.
- Jobs that have a significant amount of information to analyze.

2.11.3 Unlikely Candidates for Business Automation

The following jobs are unlikely candidates for business automation. These jobs could be too difficult or too costly to automate. The technology itself may not be mature enough to implement.

- Jobs that require high-stakes decision-making, which would have a significant consequence on business operations.
- Jobs that require a great deal of interaction – especially oral communication – with a human.
- Jobs that are highly creative, resulting in output that is imaginative.
- Jobs that require troubleshooting, diagnosis, and repair of a machine.

Notes

1 Edward Y. Uechi (2020) *Public Service Information Technology: The Definitive Manager's Guide to Harnessing Technology for Cost-Effective Operations and Services* (New York: Routledge/Productivity Press), pp. 10–12.
2 Uechi, pp. 9–20.
3 Alan S. Brown (2011) "Mechatronics and the Role of Engineers," 12 August 2011, *ASME*. <www.asme.org/topics-resources/content/mechatronics-and-the-role-of-engineers> Ken Ryan (2011) "Factory Automation: Mechatronics: A Vertical Perspective," January/February, *InTech Magazine*.
4 Ryan.
5 Kristin Lewotsky (2007) "Serving Up Better Servos," 17 January, *Motion Control Online*. <www.motioncontrolonline.org/content-detail.cfm/Motion-Control-Technical-Features/Serving-Up-Better-Servos/content_id/66>
6 Motion Control Online Marketing Team (2019) "Servo Motors Explained and Why They're Useful in Robotics," 2 July, *Motion Control Online*. <www.motioncontrolonline.org/blog-article.cfm/Servo-Motors-Explained-and-Why-They-re-Useful-in-Robotics/87>
7 National Institute of Biomedical Imaging and Bioengineering (2016) "Sensors," October. <www.nibib.nih.gov/science-education/science-topics/sensors>
8 Mark Hopkinson (2015) "With Silicon Pushed to Its Limits, What Will Power the Next Electronics Revolution?" 27 August, *Phys.org*.
9 Samuel Gibbs (2015) "Moore's Law Wins: New Chips Have Circuits 10,000 Times Thinner Than Hairs," 9 July, *The Guardian*.
10 Jesus de La Fuente, "Properties of Graphene," *Graphenea*; Gao Yang et al. (2018) "Structure of Graphene and Its Disorders: A Review," 29 August, *Science and Technology of Advanced Materials*, 19, no. 1.
11 Alessandra Lanzara (2015) "Graphene Gets a Good Gap," 21 September, *Physics*, 8, no. 91.

12 Lauren K. Wolf (2013) "The Nanotube Computer Has Arrived: Electronics: Carbon-based Alternative to Silicon Circuitry Runs Programs and Executes Instructions," 26 September, *Chemical & Engineering News*.

13 John Wenz (2019) "Why This New 16-Bit Carbon Nanotube Processor Is Such a Big Deal: Scientists Just Created a Carbon Nanotube Chip, but What Are Carbon Nanotubes Exactly?" 28 August, *Popular Mechanics*. <www.popular mechanics.com/technology/a28838017/what-are-ca>

14 Ananth Dodabalapur (2006) "Organic and Polymer Transistors for Electronics," April, *Materials Today*, 9, no. 4.

15 Stuart Hannah et al. (2018) "Multifunctional Sensor Based on Organic Field-effect Transistor and Ferroelectric Poly(vinylidene fluoride trifluoroethylene)," 30 January, *Organic Electronics*, 56.

16 Thamarasee Jeewandara (2019) "Stretchable, Self-healing and Semiconducting Polymer Films for Electronic Skin (e-skin)," 15 November. <https://phys.org/news/2019-11-stretchable-self-healing-semiconducting-polymer-electronic.html>

17 Ting Lei et al. (2017) "Biocompatible and Totally Disintegrable Semiconducting Polymer for Ultrathin and Ultralightweight Transient Electronics," 16 May, *PNAS*, 114, no. 20.

18 Phys.org (2004) "World's First Commercialization of Mercury-Free Silver Oxide Battery," 29 September. <https://phys.org/news/2004-09-world-commercialization-mercury-free-silver-oxide.html>

19 Shanhai Ge et al. (2020) "A New Approach to Both High Safety and High Performance of Lithium-ion Batteries," 28 February, *Science Advances*, 6, no. 9.

20 Phys.org (2020) "Replacing Lithium with Sodium in Batteries," 17 July. <https://phys.org/news/2020-07-lithium-sodium-batteries.html>

21 Phys.org (2020) "New Nano-engineering Strategy Shows Potential for Improved Advanced Energy Storage," 6 July. <https://phys.org/news/2020-07-nano-engineering-strategy-potential-advanced-energy.html>

22 John E. Ferguson and A. David Redish (2011) "Wireless Communication with Implanted Medical Devices Using the Conductive Properties of the Body," July, *Expert Review of Medical Devices*, 8, no. 4.

23 Seungyong Han et al. (2018) "Battery-free, Wireless Sensors for Full-body Pressure and Temperature Mapping," 4 April, *Science Translational Medicine*.

24 Jiangqi Zhao et al. (2019) "A Fully Integrated and Self-Powered Smartwatch for Continuous Sweat Glucose Monitoring," *ACS Sens*, 4, no. 7.

25 G. Traverso et al. (2015) "Physiologic Status Monitoring via the Gastrointestinal Tract," 18 November, *PLoS ONE*, 10, no. 11.

26 DNA is deoxyribonucleic acid.

27 Phys.org (2018) "Built for Speed: DNA Nanomachines Take a (Rapid) Step Forward," 7 May. <https://phys.org/news/2018-05-built-dna-nanomachines-rapid.html>

28 Hyojin Kim, Daniel Bojar, and Martin Fussenegger (2019) "A CRISPR/Cas9-based Central Processing Unit to Program Complex Logic Computation in Human Cells," 9 April, *PNAS*, 116, no. 15.

29 Merriam-Webster, "Data," *Merriam-Webster.com Dictionary*.

30 New World Encyclopedia Contributors (2019) "Abacus," 13 October, *New World Encyclopedia*.

31 John W. Tukey (1961) "The Future of Data Analysis," Research sponsored by the U.S. Army Research Office, Contract DA36–034-ORD-2297 with Princeton University, 1 July. *Princeton University and Bell Telephone Laboratories*. Preserved by the Institute of Mathematical Statistics and JSTOR.

32 David Donoho (2017) "50 Years of Data Science," 19 December, *Journal of Computational and Graphical Statistics*, 26, no. 4.

33 A. M. Turing (1950) "I. – Computing Machinery and Intelligence," October, *Mind*, LIX, no. 236, p. 442.

34 Suzana Herculano-Houzel (2009) "The Human Brain in Numbers: A Linearly Scaled-up Primate Brain," 9 November, *Frontiers in Human Neuroscience*, 3, no. 31; Roberto Lent et al. (2011) "How Many Neurons Do You Have? Some Dogmas of Quantitative Neuroscience under Revision," 13 December, *European Journal of Neuroscience*, 35, no. 1.

35 National Institute of Neurological Disorders and Stroke (2019) "Brain Basics: The Life and Death of a Neuron," 16 December. <www.ninds.nih.gov/ Disorders/Patient-Caregiver-Education/Life-and-Death-Neuron>

36 Selmer Bringsjord and Naveen Sundar Govindarajulu (2018) "Artificial Intelligence," 12 July, *The Stanford Encyclopedia of Philosophy*.

37 Turing, p. 459.

38 Turing, p. 459.

39 Thomas H. Davenport and Rajeev Ronanki (2018) "Artificial Intelligence for the Real World," January–February, *Harvard Business Review*.

40 Davenport and Ronanki.

41 BBC News (2019) "First Image of Einstein's 'Spooky' Particle Entanglement," 13 July, *BBC*.

42 Martin Giles (2019) "Explainer: What is a Quantum Computer? How It Works, Why It's So Powerful, and Where It's Likely to Be Most Useful First," 29 January, *MIT Technology Review*.

43 Giles.

44 Ruqian Wu (2018) "What's the Noise Eating Quantum Bits?" 6 January, *U.S. Department of Energy, Office of Science*.

Chapter 3

Automation in Agriculture

3.1 Chapter Summary

Chapter 3 describes the agriculture industry sector and the demand for human workers in agriculture. An historical overview of technological systems in the past is provided. This background of past systems transitions to a review of future technological systems. Based on what has been developed, I predict which future systems would be available in the near and distant future. The chapter concludes with occupations that would be affected and unaffected by business automation brought on by the technological systems designed for the agriculture sector.

3.2 Description of the Industry

The agriculture industry sector includes forestry, fishing, and hunting. Its formal name is the "Agriculture, Forestry, Fishing, and Hunting" sector. This industry covers organizations that produce products from plants, trees, fish, and animals. According to the North American Industry Classification System, businesses in this sector "grow crops, raise animals, harvest timber, and harvest fish and other animals."[1] Products may be consumed as food either raw or processed. For example, apples are picked at an orchard and transported to a grocery store, where consumers will buy and eat the apples. In another example, string beans may be harvested at a farm and shipped to a food processor, where the beans are washed, cut, cooked, and canned. Other products may be manufactured into completely new products. For example, several tons of cotton from a farm would be processed

DOI: 10.4324/9781003189329-4

into a fabric from which another industry can make clothes. Felled trees would be cut into lumber, which can be used by the construction industry. Agriculture is an industry sector whose raw products can have many uses in other industry sectors.

Businesses in this sector are commonly known as farms and ranches. They may go by other names such as vineyards, dairy farms, and fish hatcheries. These businesses use available land or water resources to grow, harvest, or otherwise manage their products. In this regard, the land or water is a critical input resource in business operation. A business in this sector may be run by a family or operated by a corporation. It may also be established as a non-profit organization.

3.3 Demand for Human Workers

In 2019, the agriculture sector employed an estimated 430,720 people across the United States, filling 136 occupations as diverse as accountants, cleaners, mechanics, truck drivers, and aircraft pilots.[2] Among the top 25 occupations, farmworkers and laborers made up the largest occupation at 232,870 people – more than half of total agriculture employment. The second and third largest occupations had 21,110 logging equipment operators and 15,470 agricultural equipment operators, respectively. Other in-demand occupations included tractor-trailer truck drivers, hand packers, graders and sorters, and first-line supervisors. Ranked in order of estimated total agriculture employment from highest to lowest, the top 25 occupations were:

1. Farmworkers and Laborers, Crop, Nursery, and Greenhouse (SOC Code: 45–2092)
2. Logging Equipment Operators (SOC Code: 45–4022)
3. Agricultural Equipment Operators (SOC Code: 45–2091)
4. Farmworkers, Farm, Ranch, and Aquacultural Animals (SOC Code: 45–2093)
5. Heavy and Tractor-Trailer Truck Drivers (SOC Code: 53–3032)
6. Packers and Packagers, Hand (SOC Code: 53–7064)
7. Graders and Sorters, Agricultural Products (SOC Code: 45–2041)
8. First-Line Supervisors of Farming, Fishing, and Forestry Workers (SOC Code: 45–1011)
9. Laborers and Freight, Stock, and Material Movers, Hand (SOC Code: 53–7062)

10. Office Clerks, General (SOC Code: 43–9061)
11. Industrial Truck and Tractor Operators (SOC Code: 53–7051)
12. Packaging and Filling Machine Operators and Tenders (SOC Code: 51–9111)
13. Secretaries and Administrative Assistants, Except Legal, Medical, and Executive (SOC Code: 43–6014)
14. General and Operations Managers (SOC Code: 11–1021)
15. Animal Caretakers (SOC Code: 39–2021)
16. Fallers (SOC Code: 45–4021)
17. Bookkeeping, Accounting, and Auditing Clerks (SOC Code: 43–3031)
18. Logging Workers, All Other (SOC Code: 45–4029)
19. Maintenance and Repair Workers, General (SOC Code: 49–9071)
20. Farmers, Ranchers, and Other Agricultural Managers (SOC Code: 11–9013)
21. Farm Equipment Mechanics and Service Technicians (SOC Code: 49–3041)
22. Inspectors, Testers, Sorters, Samplers, and Weighers (SOC Code: 51–9061)
23. Pesticide Handlers, Sprayers, and Applicators, Vegetation (SOC Code: 37–3012)
24. Animal Trainers (SOC Code: 39–2011)
25. Janitors and Cleaners, Except Maids and Housekeeping Cleaners (SOC Code: 37–2011)

Of the 136 occupations, 99 occupations were common among six or more industry sectors, making up close to 90 percent of total agriculture employment. These common occupations are important to note. In the event of a mass layoff, people hired in the 99 occupations could take their knowledge and skills and apply them in another industry sector. For example, tractor-trailer truck drivers, if they could no longer haul agricultural products, they could move to construction, manufacturing, or another industry to haul a different type of product. Several occupations were among the top 25 listed above. Other common occupations included those that dealt with standard business functions (e.g., finance, accounting, sales, marketing, and human resources).

3.4 Technological Systems in the Past

In the earlier days, horses, mules, and other animals were used to pull equipment and to carry supplies and materials. The steam engine made its way into agriculture. On the west coast of the United States, Benjamin Holt (co-founder of Caterpillar) demonstrated his steam traction engine designed to help farmers. His machine powered by a steam engine used a continuous track system to move across land. Alvin Lombard, on the east coast of the United States, designed another steam-powered continuous track machine for loggers. The Lombard Steam Log Hauler provided a way to carry many logs over land. Previously, logs were floated down rivers. The tracked-wheels provided the traction that the Holt and Lombard vehicles needed to move freely across rough terrain – especially soft soil – where wheeled vehicles would have more difficulty to maneuver through.

The traction engine was changed to use the internal combustion engine. In 1902, Charles Hart and Charles Parr began to manufacture their gasoline-powered Hart–Parr tractors. Usage of the term "traction engine" would be simplified to the word, "tractor," which was first coined by Hart and Parr.[3] In 1917, Henry Ford and Son produced its Fordson tractors. These gasoline-powered tractors, which eventually were sold the most, had larger rear wheels for power and smaller front wheels for steering.

A power take-off device would be added to a tractor model in the 1920s to transfer power from the engine to an implement connected at the rear of the tractor. A diesel-powered engine would be introduced in the 1930s. During this same decade, rubber tires were used on one particular tractor, and tests showed that rubber wheels improved fuel efficiency and made for a comfortable ride.[4] Previously, tractors had steel wheels. Also in this decade, a hydraulic draft control system was incorporated in a tractor model to raise and lower a connected implement at a certain depth in the soil.

Farm implements were redesigned and produced. Various automatic balers were designed to gather hay and shape it into a rectangular cube or a roll and to tie each bundle with twine or wire. In one estimate, one person could bale 35 to 40 tons of hay in a day with the baler.[5] Other equipment included a self-propelled harvest combine, a center pivot irrigation machine, and a gyral air seeder. One cotton combine would have replaced 80 farmworkers.[6]

The combine was a major advancement next to the tractor. It performed five functions in a single automatic process. Without the combine, numerous farmworkers were needed to thresh the harvested crop by hand. Earlier models were quickly developed for wheat and small grains. It would take a longer time to design a combine that can handle corn, because of the tougher stalks and the difficulty to pull the kernels away from the plant.

The transition from draft animals to tractors significantly increased harvest yield on existing land. Bruce Gardner, who analyzed the decline of horses and the rise of tractors, estimated that the power of one tractor was equivalent to the power of five horses or mules.[7] Reliance on animals required a dedicated portion of fields to grow crops to feed the horses and mules. With animals no longer needed, that portion of the land can be used to grow crops for human consumption. In the past when horses were used, the rows between plants could not be narrower than the width of the horse (40 to 42 inches). Sufficient space was needed for horses to move through without damaging the plants. With the design of tractors, plant rows can be closer together from 30 to 28 inches apart, which allowed for more rows in a field and thus the potential for more crops to be harvested.

The use of farm implements also increased productivity in managing farm fields. A horse-drawn plow was limited to working one plant row at a time. Mechanical implements such as plows, harrows, and planters were designed to work two rows to up to eight rows at a time.

3.5 Technological Systems in the Future

One hundred sixteen (116) start-up companies developed as many as 198 technology solutions in agriculture from 1997 to 2018 with most of the companies starting in 2013.[8] Among 213 projects funded from 2008 to 2018, the U.S. Department of Agriculture (USDA) supported innovations in mechanical harvesting and processing, sensors, remote sensing drones, machinery automation, and precision agriculture.[9] The overwhelming majority of USDA projects focused on hardware. The USDA had funded just 11 software projects related to machine learning and data analysis.

John Deere, a well-known brand in tractors, has invested resources to equip its tractors and other farm equipment with a computer, sensors, and wireless technology. This marriage of the computer and a conventional farm machine makes further advancement in the area called precision agriculture. The objective of precision agriculture is to apply inputs (e.g., seeds and chemicals) in the soil exactly where and when they are needed and in an amount that is most effective. A John Deere planting machine, for example, can plant seeds within 3 centimeters.[10] John Deere is one of several companies that is developing computerized farm machines to improve the accuracy of farming.

Advancements in farm implements have been made in terms of how accurate the implement can spread inputs. In the past, a mechanized implement would broadcast fertilizer or other farm input all around the field or disburse the input in a uniform manner without any regard to environmental conditions. Variable rate technology enables a computerized implement to disburse a specific amount in one area of the field and to disburse a different amount in another area, based on environmental conditions. Sensors in the implement analyze collected weather, soil, and other data at the precise location to determine how much should be released from the tank containing the input. Variable rate implements are particularly effective in spreading fertilizers and spraying pesticides, since the machine can precisely control how much to use.

Agco is another company that has developed a fleet of autonomous vehicles designed to carry out high-precision tasks for planting and spreading fertilizers. This is one example where multiple identical autonomous vehicles are orchestrated to operate in a swarm. Instead of operating one vehicle, many vehicles could be controlled and monitored. Working in harmony, this swarm of autonomous vehicles would be able to cover a farm field more efficiently than what a single vehicle could do. Implementation of so-called swarm vehicles is still an experiment that may not be ready for practical use.

Small motorized vehicles equipped with a computer, a sensor, and a robotic arm or some kind of mechanism to handle the plants are being developed and tested. These machines would navigate through the plant rows. A weeding machine uses a laser and two cameras to guide its way through the rows. A cutting tool attached to the machine would remove any weed that has been detected in the machine's path. Another weeding machine designed specifically for lettuce sprays a precise amount of herbicide to remove weeds and to thin overgrown areas. A pruning machine designed specifically for grapes moves through a vineyard, detecting the growth of vines and pruning excess vines where detected.

Other new machines cover the areas of pesticide application and irrigation management. Machines to aid in crop harvesting, which is very labor intensive, are being developed for specialty crops such as apples, strawberries, broccoli, and cauliflower. A self-propelled apple harvester operates in the field where picked apples can be immediately sorted. A robotic machine has been developed to detect the ripeness of strawberries and to remove the ripened fruit from the plants. Another harvesting machine has been designed to pick broccoli and cauliflower. All of these machines have been tested on a small number of farms.

A challenge in scaling harvesting machines is in the ability to handle different crops. Agriculture has a wide range of products that include grains, oilseeds, vegetables, and fruits. Each product can have unique characteristics in color, texture, hardness, and as it grows over time. A tomato, for example, changes color as it grows and ripens on the vine. As such, one machine designed for one crop would not work for another crop. For example, a strawberry harvester would not work to pick apples. A harvesting machine may be able to be reconfigured and reprogrammed for another product, but such a change will involve additional time and testing. Innovations in harvesting machines cover a few specific crops. It will take several more years for more machines to be available that can harvest all other crops.

An unmanned aerial vehicle (UAV, also known as a drone) is another advanced technology that is being used in agriculture. This is a remote-controlled aircraft with a computer, a camera, and a network device. It is primarily used as a scout to identify changing conditions in the field. As it flies over the field, the UAV captures and transmits images of specific areas of the field. Various UAV designs would be able to indicate soil moisture, nutrient content, or plant growth. In the past, a team of human scouts would go out to the field and observe and record conditions. Now, this work can be done with a drone.

An innovation worth mentioning is vertical farming. This new form takes farming indoors. Instead of growing plants across acres of land, plants can be grown vertically in stacks inside a building. Vertical farming uses hydroponics, which is a method of growing plants without soil. Plants are grown in a water-based solution. Start-up companies have incorporated computers, sensors, robotics, and unique lighting to create a controlled environment that monitors the growth of plants. Current vertical farming is limited to producing leafy-green vegetables (e.g., lettuce).

3.6 Forecasting of Technological Systems

Vertical farming, computerized tractors, and variable rate implements are available now. Though, the costs of these new technological systems can be high. They would be cost-effective for large-scale businesses. The smaller businesses may not be able to afford the technologies. Calculating the costs of the machines and workers as described in Chapter 1 and comparing the costs will determine whether an organization of any size can and should use the technological systems.

UAVs are also available now. This particular technology would be less expensive than the computerized tractors and variable rate implements.

Within the next 7 years, motorized machines related to planting, weeding, pruning, chemical application, and water management would be available. These machines could apply to a wide range of agricultural products. Any modification to fit a particular crop would likely not take a long time. Specialized harvesting machines for apples, strawberries, broccoli, and other crops that have passed thorough testing could be available in this time period.

From 8 to 15 years, additional harvesting machines designed for other crops may be available. This prediction assumes that engineers have chosen the selected crops for development and testing. At the later end of this time period (12–15 years), swarm vehicles may be rolled out into production for practical use.

From 16 to 25 years in the future, swarm vehicles would likely have matured. There could be autonomous vehicles moving across farm fields to do certain tasks at any time day or night.

3.7 Changes in Jobs, Roles, and Occupations

Farmworkers and laborers, graders and sorters, and pesticide applicators will be affected the most by future technological systems. These occupations could be eliminated or likely see a substantial decrease in employment.

Equipment operators and mechanics would be unaffected by the new technologies. Agricultural businesses will still need people who know how to operate and repair the computerized machines. What will definitely change is the skills of existing operators and mechanics. They will be required to understand how the technologies work. The job of operators and mechanics will change in the type of machine that they will be working with – from a purely mechanical machine to a computerized machine that uses mechanical engineering, electronics, and computer software.

The role of first-line supervisors will shift from supervising people to managing machines. With machines replacing farmworkers, first-line supervisors would have the responsibility to ensure that the machines are functioning properly in the field. They would call a mechanic in the event of a malfunction. On day-to-day operation, they would check the machine, load it with inputs, and keep it clean and safe from the elements.

The role of agricultural managers may not be impacted as much and would likely remain unchanged. Agricultural managers will still oversee and manage operations, albeit with a higher number of machines compared to the number of human workers. Given that machines can operate 24 hours a day, agricultural managers would need to oversee operations around the clock – not just from dawn to dusk.

An additional job that agricultural managers and first-line supervisors will have to do relates to data analysis. Data from the tractors, implements, UAVs, and autonomous vehicles will pour into the organization's operations. A range of decisions on any given day will have to be made. Managers and supervisors will need to have the analytical skill to review all the data that come in.

Based on an analysis of a sample of 2019 employment data from the Bureau of Labor Statistics, 63.8 percent of human workers in the agriculture sector would be displaced by business automation brought on by future technological systems. A small proportion of human workers (13.1 percent) would be unaffected by the new systems. The following six occupations would be unaffected by future technological systems:

1. Logging Equipment Operators (SOC Code: 45–4022)
2. Agricultural Equipment Operators (SOC Code: 45–2091)
3. First-Line Supervisors of Farming, Fishing, and Forestry Workers (SOC Code: 45–1011)
4. Maintenance and Repair Workers, General (SOC Code: 49–9071)
5. Farmers, Ranchers, and Other Agricultural Managers (SOC Code: 11–9013)
6. Farm Equipment Mechanics and Service Technicians (SOC Code: 49–3041)

On the other hand, the following five occupations would be affected by future technological systems:

1. Farmworkers and Laborers, Crop, Nursery, and Greenhouse (SOC Code: 45–2092)
2. Farmworkers, Farm, Ranch, and Aquacultural Animals (SOC Code: 45–2093)
3. Packers and Packagers, Hand (SOC Code: 53–7064)
4. Graders and Sorters, Agricultural Products (SOC Code: 45–2041)
5. Pesticide Handlers, Sprayers, and Applicators, Vegetation (SOC Code: 37–3012)

Notes

1 U.S. Bureau of Labor Statistics (2021) "Industries at a Glance: Agriculture, Forestry, Fishing and Hunting: NAICS 11," 8 January, *U.S. Department of Labor, Bureau of Labor Statistics*. <www.bls.gov/iag/tgs/iag11.htm>

2 U.S. Bureau of Labor Statistics (2019) "Occupational Employment Statistics (OES) Survey," May 2019 OES Estimates, *U.S. Department of Labor, Bureau of Labor Statistics.*

3 National Academy of Engineering, "Agricultural Mechanization Timeline," *Greatest Engineering Achievements.* Adapted from the book: George Constable and Bob Somerville (2003) *A Century of Innovation: Twenty Engineering Achievements That Transformed Our Lives* (Washington, DC: Joseph Henry Press).

4 National Academy of Engineering.

5 Bill Ganzel, "Haying Equipment during the 1940s," *Wessels Living History Farm.* <https://livinghistoryfarm.org/farminginthe40s/machines_06.html>

6 Bill Ganzel (2007) "Cotton Harvesting during the 1950s and 60s," *Wessels Living History Farm.* <https://livinghistoryfarm.org/farminginthe50s/machines_15.html>

7 Bill Ganzel, "Horses Finally Lose Their Jobs on the Farm during the 1940s," *Wessels Living History Farm.* <https://livinghistoryfarm.org/farminginthe40s/machines_13.html>

8 Julian Schirmer et al. (2021) "Emerging Innovation Patterns in Digital Agriculture: A Study of 198 Digital Solutions from 116 Startups," Proceedings of the 54th Hawaii International Conference on System Sciences, 5 January, *University of Hawaii, Hamilton Library.*

9 Gregory Astill, Agnes Perez, and Suzanne Thornsbury (2020) "Developing Automation and Mechanization for Specialty Crops: A Review of U.S. Department of Agriculture Programs," Report to Congress, AP-082, February 2020, *U.S. Department of Agriculture, Economic Research Service.*

10 Wincent (2016) "iSow and iReap – The Automation and Digitization of Farming," 18 November, *Harvard Business School, Digital Initiative.* <https://digital.hbs.edu/platform-rctom/submission/isow-and-ireap-the-automation-and-digitization-of-farming/#>

Chapter 4

Automation in Manufacturing

4.1 Chapter Summary

Chapter 4 describes the manufacturing industry sector and the demand for human workers in manufacturing. An historical overview of technological systems in the past is provided. This background of past systems transitions to a review of future technological systems. Based on what has been developed, I predict which future systems would be available in the near and distant future. The chapter concludes with occupations that would be affected and unaffected by business automation brought on by the technological systems designed for the manufacturing sector.

4.2 Description of the Industry

The manufacturing industry sector covers organizations that produce new products from raw and manufactured products. According to the North American Industry Classification System, businesses in this sector transform materials, substances, or components through a mechanical, physical, or chemical process to develop new products demanded by customers.[1] This broad definition encompasses a wide range of enterprises from makers of consumable goods to makers of durable goods. A bakery, for example, is considered a manufacturer, since it is a business that takes flour, sugar, and other ingredients to create bread and pastries for sale. Another manufacturer completely unrelated to baking takes steel, plastic, rubber, pre-fabricated

DOI: 10.4324/9781003189329-5

bolts, and other materials to build automobiles. Another type of manufacturer experiments with chemicals and plant extracts to develop new kinds of drugs. In all of these examples, the organizations use machines and specialized equipment and a particular process to develop their products. They purchase materials or substances from other organizations and use those purchased goods in their machines. Manufacturing is a sector that relies on acquiring raw or manufactured products that had been produced from another industry sector.

Businesses in this sector are commonly known as plants, factories, and mills. They would all be registered companies, as some level of risk to safety and health is involved in making their products. These organizations would have a governance structure and a management team to plan and oversee operations. The cost of starting the business can be relatively high. The cost of maintaining the business may be high, due to recurring costs to replenish stocks of materials.

4.3 Demand for Human Workers

In 2019, the manufacturing sector employed an estimated 12.71 million people across the United States, filling 535 various occupations.[2] Among the top 25 occupations, miscellaneous assemblers and fabricators made up the largest occupation at more than 1 million people. The second and third largest occupations had 462,950 first-line supervisors and 365,290 inspectors, testers, and sorters, respectively. Other in-demand occupations included material movers, machinists, machine operators, welders, solderers, and electrical assemblers. Ranked in order of estimated total manufacturing employment from highest to lowest, the top 25 occupations were:

1. Miscellaneous Assemblers and Fabricators (SOC Code: 51–2090)
2. First-Line Supervisors of Production and Operating Workers (SOC Code: 51–1011)
3. Inspectors, Testers, Sorters, Samplers, and Weighers (SOC Code: 51–9061)
4. Laborers and Freight, Stock, and Material Movers, Hand (SOC Code: 53–7062)
5. Machinists (SOC Code: 51–4041)
6. Packaging and Filling Machine Operators and Tenders (SOC Code: 51–9111)

7. Welders, Cutters, Solderers, and Brazers (SOC Code: 51–4121)
8. Electrical, Electronic, and Electromechanical Assemblers, Except Coil Winders, Tapers, and Finishers (SOC Code: 51–2028)
9. Sales Representatives, Wholesale and Manufacturing, Except Technical and Scientific Products (SOC Code: 41–4012)
10. General and Operations Managers (SOC Code: 11–1021)
11. Industrial Machinery Mechanics (SOC Code: 49–9041)
12. Shipping, Receiving, and Inventory Clerks (SOC Code: 43–5071)
13. Industrial Engineers (SOC Code: 17–2112)
14. Maintenance and Repair Workers, General (SOC Code: 49–9071)
15. Helpers – Production Workers (SOC Code: 51–9198)
16. Cutting, Punching, and Press Machine Setters, Operators, and Tenders, Metal and Plastic (SOC Code: 51–4031)
17. Industrial Truck and Tractor Operators (SOC Code: 53–7051)
18. Molding, Coremaking, and Casting Machine Setters, Operators, and Tenders, Metal and Plastic (SOC Code: 51–4072)
19. Office Clerks, General (SOC Code: 43–9061)
20. Packers and Packagers, Hand (SOC Code: 53–7064)
21. Software Developers and Software Quality Assurance Analysts and Testers (SOC Code: 15–1256)
22. Mechanical Engineers (SOC Code: 17–2141)
23. Customer Service Representatives (SOC Code: 43–4051)
24. Computer Numerically Controlled Tool Operators (SOC Code: 51–9161)
25. Industrial Production Managers (SOC Code: 11–3051)

Of the 535 occupations, 248 occupations were common among six or more industry sectors, making up more than 9 million of total manufacturing employment. These common occupations are important to note. In the event of a mass layoff, people hired in the 248 occupations could take their knowledge and skills and apply them in another industry sector. For example, laborers and material movers, if they found themselves unemployed, could move to the transportation and warehousing sector, the administrative and support sector, or another industry where they can apply their same skills. The top seven common occupations were among the top 25 occupations. Other common occupations included software developers, computer systems analysts, information systems managers, mechanical engineers, customer service representatives, tractor-trailer truck drivers, and stockers and order fillers.

Less in demand were nine occupations unique to the manufacturing sector. In this sector, semiconductor processing technicians and patternmakers were hired. Businesses in other industry sectors did not have people employed in these occupations.

4.4 Technological Systems in the Past

Before the industrial revolution, products were made by hand by craftsmen and artists. Tools were used but they were powered by hand. Examples of hand tools included a hand plane, a hand-cranked drill, and a hand saw. The construction of a single unit of product would have been painstakingly slow, as one person would take the necessary time to handcraft each product one by one. The finished product, therefore, resulted in a unique piece that would have been slightly different from the previous piece that was constructed. No two items of the same model could have been 100 percent identical.

A large number of firearms would have been needed to win a war in the 18th century. But building muskets by hand proved inadequate in order to produce a high number in a short period of time. To solve this productivity problem: a French gunsmith named Honoré LeBlanc developed the concept of interchangeable parts.[3] He came up with the idea of constructing the individual parts of a gun to be identical. The identical parts can then be fitted in a standardized way. This would allow a craftsman to assemble a firearm in faster time. It would also allow a broken musket to be repaired by replacing the necessary part. With a government contract to produce muskets, Eli Whitney seized on this idea and managed to produce 10,000 muskets as required.[4] The concept of interchangeable parts would be a key part in future manufacturing.

In a detailed government report published in 1886, it was estimated that three workers were able to produce 125 to 150 muskets in a day by using specialized machines and a division of labor scheme.[5] Specific tasks were divided up among a team of workers, instead of depending on any one person to carry out all tasks. It would have taken one worker with the use of hand tools to produce one musket in a day.

Interchangeable parts and division of labor were incorporated in the assembly line concept. Ransom Olds, founder of the Olds Motor Vehicle Company, managed to produce the Oldsmobile Curved Dash model at a rate of 20 per day,[6] by mounting the body on a wooden frame with wheels and pulling it from station to station where a worker at each station added parts. Ten years later, Henry Ford improved the assembly line by using a conveyor system to move the vehicle faster. He was able to produce the Model T at a rate of one every 90 minutes.[7]

The individual stations in the automotive assembly line would be further improved in the 1960s by installing large mechanical arms.

As early as the 1930s, industrial control systems were used to manage operations of power plants, oil refineries, chemical processing plants, and electricity transmission stations. Various names went by SCADA (Supervisory Control and Data Acquisition), DCS (Distributed Control System), and PCS (Process Control System). The industrial control system would have either a closed-loop feedback control or an open-loop feedback control. In an open-loop feedback control, the system would indicate a change in operation, and the human operator would react appropriately to the change as indicated. For example, a human operator would see an error light turn on and would then press a switch or turn a valve. In a closed-loop feedback control, a sensor detects a change and sends the change to a controller. The controller in turn makes an adjustment according to a computer software program written to handle the detected change. A human operator is not involved in the closed-loop feedback control. Earlier analog systems used relays, valves, and pneumatic gauges. Later digital systems used a computer and electronics.

4.5 Technological Systems in the Future

Additive manufacturing (also known as 3D printing) is an innovative process in which an object can be made layer by layer with such high degree of precision that allows the object to conform to hitherto new geometric shapes. The material used to make the object can be plastic, metal, or concrete. In the past, wood or plastic models were made into molds. The molds were then made into metal castings from which the finished products were produced. Additive manufacturing removes the steps to produce molds, going directly from conceptual design to finished product. The process would start with a computer-aided design (CAD) drawing of the product. The CAD drawing would then be sent to the 3D printer, which outputs the object layer by layer according to the specifications in the CAD drawing. Then the 3D printer would be able to replicate production by printing a number of copies of the object.

Autonomous trucks are being manufactured by Caterpillar and Komatsu to increase productivity and improve safety in mining.[8] These massive heavy trucks would be able to operate 24 hours a day in hazardous mining areas without a human driver. Given the environment of a mine, they would be able to travel on dusty unpaved roads at various inclines, stopping, starting, turning, and maneuvering around. Caterpillar's autonomous driving technology, which comprises computer hardware and software and remote-control operation, can be fitted in a conventional heavy truck.[9] A key distinction in this kind of autonomous vehicle is that it is teleoperated. While a human driver is not present in the truck, a human still controls the truck from an office located somewhere else. The human worker is operating the truck by remote control.

Automatic guided vehicles allow materials and goods to be moved around without a human operator. In the past, a worker drove a forklift to move a pallet through a warehouse. A worker also used a pallet jack to haul a pallet. Automatic guided vehicles modernize the forklift and pallet jack with a computer, a sensor, and a method of navigation. A vehicle can be guided around the warehouse floor by wire, magnetic tape, magnetic bar, laser, or another method designed by the manufacturer of the vehicle. A computer software program instructs a vehicle where to go. A constraint with this technology is that the automatic guided vehicle follows a pre-defined process and a fixed route.

Similar to the automatic guided vehicle, an autonomous mobile robot moves inventory around the facility. But the key difference is in its flexibility to move freely. The autonomous mobile robot is equipped with maps and multiple sensors to be able to learn from where it has traveled and to reroute its path to avoid obstacles. This technological system is not constrained by a fixed route.

An automatic palletizer moves cases of product from a conveyor system to a pallet, layer by layer. Once it completes stacking the cases in a number of layers on the pallet, the automatic palletizer applies stretch wrap to seal all layers of cases to the pallet. This machine can stack cases, cartons, boxes, or whatever container is used to package the individual products. Previously, a human worker had to lift and neatly stack the boxes by hand.

A collaborative robot or a co-bot is a robotic machine designed to work alongside a human worker. It is not intended to replace a human. A co-bot leverages the strengths of both machine and human. The machine, on one hand, provides the power to lift a heavy object and yet offers the dexterity to handle a small delicate item. The human, on the other hand, has the reasoning ability to guide the machine in what to do. The co-bot may be a robotic arm equipped with a computer, a servo motor, and a sensor. It would be programmed to carry out a repetitive task. The co-bot may be used in fabrication, assembly, or inspection. One particular manufacturer developed a portable co-bot with two arms that has the ability to handle electronic parts.[10]

A computer numerical control (CNC) machine modernizes a machine tool such as a milling machine, a lathe, and a router. A computer executes instructions to cut wood, metal, or another material very precisely with little waste. The computer software program is written in a specialized language called G-code. A wide range of CNC machines can be made with a cutter that can handle a specific type of material (e.g., a laser cutter or a plasma cutter). The CNC machine can be small to fit on a table or large to fill a room.

With a combination of automatic guided vehicles, autonomous mobile robots, automatic palletizers, and co-bots, a factory floor could operate without human workers. And if such an environment does not have people, the operating environment could eliminate overhead lighting. A computerized machine does not necessarily need light to see the work in a way that a human needs light to see his work. "Lights-out manufacturing" is a novel concept where all of the automated machines operate in the dark. Two companies in Japan and China have implemented this approach. The Chinese company managed to reduce its staff from 500 workers to an essential team of 5 technicians.[11] In addition to reducing the cost of labor, lights-out manufacturing can also reduce the cost of energy usage.

4.6 Forecasting of Technological Systems

All of the technological systems except for autonomous trucks and collaborative robots are available now. Depending on particular business needs, organizations will need to evaluate how each system can contribute to operations. In certain cases, combining two or more of the systems will be effective. Just using one type of automatic machine may not make sense. For example, once an automatic palletizer has completed wrapping a pallet of goods, an autonomous guided vehicle can take the pallet and load it on a truck. Without the autonomous guided vehicle, a human operator with a forklift or pallet jack would be needed. Likewise, without the automatic palletizer, a number of human workers would be needed to stack boxes on the pallet. Having both types of machines will increase productivity to prepare and move more pallets.

Within the next 7 years, autonomous trucks will be limited to particular areas where there is no commuter traffic. Autonomous trucks would operate within defined boundaries of a given space from an isolated mine to an enclosed facility. Mining is a special case. Other foreseeable cases would be in farming and forestry. The construction industry would have a viable business case for using autonomous trucks. During this same time period, collaborative robots would be limited to early adopters that have started using the technology or are trying them out in experimental form. The number of practical applications for co-bots will be relatively low. Programming co-bots will concentrate on specialized repetitive tasks.

From 8 to 15 years, collaborative robots will be further improved and programmed for a wider array of tasks. This would allow more manufacturers to adopt co-bots. Near the end of this time period (14–15 years), the technology behind autonomous trucks may be available in lighter industrial trucks (e.g., a box truck).

From 16 to 25 years in the future, light industrial trucks will be autonomous only when they are driving within the perimeter of a warehouse or other private property to load and unload goods. A human driver will still be in full control to operate the truck on public roads. During this time period, additive manufacturing will be available for large-scale applications such as that in the construction industry. Near the end of this time period (24–25 years), certain collaborative robots that have been programmed with machine learning will have the capacity for cognitive insight and the ability to make simple, inconsequential decisions. Such decisions will be limited to the scope of the task for which the co-bot has been programmed. The co-bot in this case will not have matured enough to reach cognitive engagement.

4.7 Changes in Jobs, Roles, and Occupations

Ten out of the 25 occupations listed above (40 percent) could be significantly impacted by future technological systems. Several occupations such as miscellaneous assemblers, material movers, welders and cutters, shipping and receiving clerks, production workers, molding and casting machine setters, and packers and packagers can be eliminated.

Inspectors, testers, and machinists would be occupations that could work alongside collaborative robots. These workers would shift their job focus to analysis and reasoning. While their robotic counterpart does the physical work, the human worker can concentrate on the mental part.

Machinery mechanics and maintenance and repair workers will have a higher profile in manufacturing. These occupations will be needed even more to ensure that all equipment remain operable. They will intervene whenever a machine needs to be repaired. Of course, these workers will require additional training to understand the automated machines.

The role of first-line supervisors will likely change from supervising people to managing machines. With the elimination of assemblers and production workers, the number of first-line supervisors could be reduced. It might make sense to convert this occupation into a CNC tool operator or an industrial production manager. Job responsibilities may overlap across the occupations. Merging of occupations may be warranted.

The numbers of industrial engineers, mechanical engineers, and software developers will for sure increase. These will be the workers who have the capacity to design and develop automated machines. The demand for engineers and developers will grow in future years, moving their employment rank higher from the bottom list of top-ranked occupations. The CNC tool operators and industrial production managers will also move higher in their employment rank.

Based on an analysis of a sample of 2019 employment data from the Bureau of Labor Statistics, 24.1 percent of human workers in the manufacturing sector would be displaced by business automation brought on by future technological systems. A proportion of human workers less than that who would be displaced (18.5 percent) would be unaffected by the new systems. The following ten occupations would be unaffected by future technological systems:

1. First-Line Supervisors of Production and Operating Workers (SOC Code: 51–1011)
2. Inspectors, Testers, Sorters, Samplers, and Weighers (SOC Code: 51–9061)
3. Machinists (SOC Code: 51–4041)
4. Industrial Machinery Mechanics (SOC Code: 49–9041)
5. Industrial Engineers (SOC Code: 17–2112)
6. Maintenance and Repair Workers, General (SOC Code: 49–9071)
7. Software Developers and Software Quality Assurance Analysts and Testers (SOC Code: 15–1256)

8. Mechanical Engineers (SOC Code: 17–2141)
9. Computer Numerically Controlled Tool Operators (SOC Code: 51–9161)
10. Industrial Production Managers (SOC Code: 11–3051)

On the other hand, the following ten occupations would be affected by future technological systems:

1. Miscellaneous Assemblers and Fabricators (SOC Code: 51–2090)
2. Laborers and Freight, Stock, and Material Movers, Hand (SOC Code: 53–7062)
3. Packaging and Filling Machine Operators and Tenders (SOC Code: 51–9111)
4. Welders, Cutters, Solderers, and Brazers (SOC Code: 51–4121)
5. Electrical, Electronic, and Electromechanical Assemblers, Except Coil Winders, Tapers, and Finishers (SOC Code: 51–2028)
6. Shipping, Receiving, and Inventory Clerks (SOC Code: 43–5071)
7. Helpers – Production Workers (SOC Code: 51–9198)
8. Cutting, Punching, and Press Machine Setters, Operators, and Tenders, Metal and Plastic (SOC Code: 51–4031)
9. Molding, Coremaking, and Casting Machine Setters, Operators, and Tenders, Metal and Plastic (SOC Code: 51–4072)
10. Packers and Packagers, Hand (SOC Code: 53–7064)

Notes

1 U.S. Bureau of Labor Statistics (2021) "Industries at a Glance: Manufacturing: NAICS 31–33," 8 January, *U.S. Department of Labor, Bureau of Labor Statistics.* <www.bls.gov/iag/tgs/iag31-33.htm>
2 U.S. Bureau of Labor Statistics (2019) "Occupational Employment Statistics (OES) Survey," May 2019 OES Estimates, *U.S. Department of Labor, Bureau of Labor Statistics.*
3 Robert Corday (2014) "The Evolution of Assembly Lines: A Brief History," 24 April, *Robohub.* <https://robohub.org/the-evolution-of-assembly-lines-a-brief-history/>
4 History.com Editors (2018) "Interchangeable Parts," 21 August, *History.* <www.history.com/topics/inventions/interchangeable-parts>
5 Jeremy Atack, Robert A. Margo, and Paul W. Rhode (2019) "'Automation' of Manufacturing in the Late Nineteenth Century: The Hand and Machine Labor Study," Spring 2019, *Journal of Economic Perspectives*, 33, no. 2, p. 52.
6 Corday.

7 Corday.

8 Matrix (2011) "CAT in Major Autonomous Truck Milestone with Fortescue Deal . . . while Rio Doubles Its Komatsu Driverless Fleet," 6 July, *International Mining*. <https://im-mining.com/2011/07/06/cat-in-major-autonomous-truck-milestone-with-fortescue-dealwhile-rio-doubles-its-komatsu-driverless-fleet/>

9 Rajesh Kumar Singh (2020) "Caterpillar Bets on Self-driving Machines Impervious to Pandemics," 12 October, *Reuters*. <www.reuters.com/article/idUSKBN26X1ET>

10 Erico Guizzo (2011) "ABB's FRIDA Offers Glimpse of Future Factory Robots," 19 April, *IEEE Spectrum*. <https://spectrum.ieee.org/abb-factory-robot-frida>

11 CB Insights (2019) "Future Factory: How Technology Is Transforming Manufacturing," 27 June, *CB Insights*. <www.cbinsights.com/research/future-factory-manufacturing-tech-trends/>

Chapter 5

Automation in Construction

5.1 Chapter Summary

Chapter 5 describes the construction industry sector and the demand for human workers in construction. An historical overview of technological systems in the past is provided. This background of past systems transitions to a cursory summary of future technological systems. Based on what has been developed, I predict which future systems would be available in the near and distant future. The chapter concludes with occupations that would be affected and unaffected by business automation brought on by the technological systems designed for the construction sector.

5.2 Description of the Industry

The construction industry sector covers organizations that construct buildings, reservoirs, canals, highways, and complex civil engineering projects. The end result of such projects may serve a private or public purpose. For instance, completion of a reservoir serves to provide hydro-electric power to millions of people. Completion of an interstate expressway serves to allow commercial vehicles and private cars to travel across multiple states for business and leisure. Completion of a building serves the purpose for the employees of a corporation to work in. Completion of a house serves the purpose for a family to live in.

Organizations in this sector would be dependent on time-limited contracts, which would be defined by the start and end dates of construction.

Hired workers may not be permanent employees. There may be a number of independent organizations working together through the arrangement of contracts.

5.3 Demand for Human Workers

In 2019, the construction sector employed an estimated 7.44 million people across the United States, filling 364 occupations comprised mainly of highly specialized fields.[1] Among the top 25 occupations, construction laborers made up the largest occupation at 866,650 people. The second and third largest occupations had 621,980 carpenters and 527,300 electricians, respectively. Other in-demand occupations included plumbers, pipefitters, equipment operators, heating and air-conditioning mechanics, painters, cement masons, first-line supervisors, and construction managers. Ranked in order of estimated total construction employment from highest to lowest, the top 25 occupations were:

1. Construction Laborers (SOC Code: 47–2061)
2. Carpenters (SOC Code: 47–2031)
3. Electricians (SOC Code: 47–2111)
4. First-Line Supervisors of Construction Trades and Extraction Workers (SOC Code: 47–1011)
5. Plumbers, Pipefitters, and Steamfitters (SOC Code: 47–2152)
6. Office Clerks, General (SOC Code: 43–9061)
7. Operating Engineers and Other Construction Equipment Operators (SOC Code: 47–2073)
8. Heating, Air Conditioning, and Refrigeration Mechanics and Installers (SOC Code: 49–9021)
9. Construction Managers (SOC Code: 11–9021)
10. Painters, Construction and Maintenance (SOC Code: 47–2141)
11. Cement Masons and Concrete Finishers (SOC Code: 47–2051)
12. General and Operations Managers (SOC Code: 11–1021)
13. Secretaries and Administrative Assistants, Except Legal, Medical, and Executive (SOC Code: 43–6014)
14. Roofers (SOC Code: 47–2181)
15. Cost Estimators (SOC Code: 13–1051)
16. Heavy and Tractor-Trailer Truck Drivers (SOC Code: 53–3032)
17. Bookkeeping, Accounting, and Auditing Clerks (SOC Code: 43–3031)

18. Drywall and Ceiling Tile Installers (SOC Code: 47–2081)
19. Sales Representatives of Services, Except Advertising, Insurance, Financial Services, and Travel (SOC Code: 41–3091)
20. Sheet Metal Workers (SOC Code: 47–2211)
21. Helpers – Electricians (SOC Code: 47–3013)
22. Structural Iron and Steel Workers (SOC Code: 47–2221)
23. Project Management Specialists and Business Operations Specialists, All Other (SOC Code: 13–1198)
24. Brickmasons and Blockmasons (SOC Code: 47–2021)
25. Helpers – Pipelayers, Plumbers, Pipefitters, and Steamfitters (SOC Code: 47–3015)

Of the 364 occupations, 219 occupations were common among six or more industry sectors, making up more than 80 percent of total construction employment. These common occupations are important to note. In the event of a mass layoff, people hired in the 219 occupations could take their knowledge and skills and apply them in another industry sector. For example, cost estimators, if they found themselves unemployed, could move to manufacturing, the administrative and support sector, or another industry. Given that this sector consists primarily of contractors, workers would take it as part of the job to move to wherever there are construction jobs. The top ten common occupations were among the top 25 occupations. Other common occupations included those that dealt with administrative work (e.g., operations managers, administrative assistants, cost estimators, and accounting) and sales.

5.4 Technological Systems in the Past

Hauling heavy materials across a certain distance and certain height has been an important part of construction since ancient times. Lack of written documentation, however, cannot tell what technology was used to construct the Ziggurat of Ur, the Egyptian pyramids, and the Mayan pyramids. Theories on the use of a ramp and moving stone on top of logs do not sound farfetched. For sure, a considerable labor force in the hundreds would have been required to move heavy stone and to carve solid blocks to fit together.

Artistic renderings depict an ancient Roman wooden crane that used a pulley system and a large treadwheel.[2] Illustrations show more than one person inside the treadwheel. The workers would have walked in either direction to turn the wheel, which causes the pulley system to bring an object up or down. The crane attributed to the Roman engineer Marcus Vitruvius Pollio would have been used to build various Roman structures. A reproduction of the crane at 7 meters tall showed that the crane could lift 12 tons of material.[3] The power source in this machine was human feet.

In the early 1800s, William Otis designed and patented a steam-powered shovel to aid in the construction of the railroad. His machine used a steam engine and a 1.1 cubic meter bucket in a crane configuration to move and clear away earth. The Otis steam shovel could move 380 cubic meters of earth in a day.[4] Previously, laborers with hand shovels and pickaxes were relied upon to dig and move earth.

The use of hydraulics in construction machines appeared in the mid to late 1800s when William George Armstrong manufactured and sold hydraulic cranes and other hydraulic machinery.[5] His machine relied on water pressure.

The 20th century saw the development of new and improved construction machines and power tools. Combining the continuous track system described in Chapter 3, the internal combustion engine, and hydraulics, bulldozers, backhoes, excavators, and cranes were manufactured and used. Other machines included graders, loaders, and trenchers. The crane has advanced to include a telescopic boom that with hydraulics can extend the height of the crane by two, three, or more times. A stationary tower crane is also an advancement that facilitates the construction of tall buildings at great heights. Various hand tools were electrified with a motor, so that wood can be cut, carved, and smoothed at a faster rate, holes can be drilled at a faster rate, and screws can be turned and fastened at a faster rate. Examples included a circular saw, a table saw, an electric jigsaw, an automatic sander, and a power drill with interchangeable drill bits. The pneumatic nail gun is a particular innovation that allows a worker to drive several nails into wood or other material consistently, with ease, and at a faster rate.

5.5 Technological Systems in the Future

Effort has been made since the 1980s to design and test new types of equipment that could automate construction. However, disseminating the results of research and development to industry practice has been slow.[6] A chief problem was found in the lack of attention and work to analyze, design, manage, and improve the business process of construction.[7] Before an automated device is selected and used, a business manager must review her business process, identify which part can be automated, and then evaluate what type of equipment is best suited to automate that part of the process. By integrating planning, design, fabrication, and assembly processes like in manufacturing and understanding how the processes function as a whole system, the construction industry would be able to automate.[8]

There are technologies that the construction sector can apply from other industries. From Chapter 4, additive manufacturing, computer-aided design (CAD) software, CNC machines, and autonomous trucks can be used in construction.

The following systems, machines, and robots have been designed for the construction sector[9]:

1. A teleoperated John Deere excavator (remote-control operation) designed for repairing an airport runway;
2. A teleoperated micro-tunneling machine (remote-control operation) designed to dig a tunnel for the purpose of installing a pipeline;
3. A robotic excavator and autonomous pipe mapper specially designed to avoid damaging existing utility pipes;
4. An automatic pipe bending system designed to bend and connect pipe sections;
5. An automatic slipform machine for placement of concrete sidewalks, curbs, and gutters;
6. A laser-aided grading system for automatic grading control;
7. A shear stud welder machine designed to weld shear connectors in composite steel and concrete structures;
8. A WallBot intelligent agent (developed at the Massachusetts Institute of Technology) designed to reshape and reconfigure an interior partition wall dynamically; and
9. A BlockBot robot (developed at the Massachusetts Institute of Technology) designed to operate in a swarm with numerous other BlockBot robots to create a variety of shapes and forms such as a wall or a staircase.

The following experimental machines show what could be possible in the construction sector[10]:

1. A semi-automated mason (SAM) machine designed to lay down bricks and fill in mortar at a rate of 6,000 bricks in a day;
2. A mesh maker machine designed with a robotic arm that builds a double layer of metal bars to create a wall that can be straight or curved;

3. A gantry 3D printer designed to build a concrete wall layer by layer on site; and
4. An orchestration of UAVs (or drones) operating in a swarm designed to work together to carry and build materials at a construction site.

In a situation where a human cannot be physically present, a haptic interface system can be used. This technology simulates reality by providing tactile information to the human in such a way as to enable the human to respond in a certain way. A human worker located in a remote location would operate mechanical arms or some type of apparatus connected to a computer. Another set of corresponding mechanical arms would be deployed at the actual site. A video camera records the movement of the arms and sends the video to the human worker. As the human worker moves the arms in a particular way, he will see the on-site arms move in the same way via the video display monitor. The on-site arms equipped with sensors would be programmed to detect an amount of force. He would see the amount of force displayed on the monitor and adjust his movements accordingly. A successful demonstration of a haptic interface system was performed in an underwater environment.[11]

5.6 Forecasting of Technological Systems

CNC machines, pipe bending machines, slipform pavers, laser-aided grading systems, and shear stud welder machines are available now.

Within the next 7 years, teleoperated micro-tunneling machines would be available. Teleoperated excavators would also be available during this time period. Similar to how it is explained in Chapter 4, autonomous trucks would operate within defined boundaries of construction sites. A driver would have to take full control when driving the truck on public roads.

From 8 to 15 years, a machine that combines robotic excavation and autonomous pipe mapping may be available. During this same time period, WallBot intelligent agents, semi-automated mason machines, mesh maker machines, and haptic interface systems would be available.

From 16 to 25 years in the future, additive manufacturing specifically to build 3D-printed buildings would be available. Near the end of this time period (24–25 years), BlockBot robots and swarm drones could be available.

5.7 Changes in Jobs, Roles, and Occupations

Construction laborers, the top ranked occupation, are at high risk of being displaced workers. To avoid this situation, they should consider specializing in a particular trade. Any specialized field except the occupations related to cement masons, brickmasons, roofers, painters, and drywall and ceiling tile installers can be considered. Cement masons, concrete finishers, brickmasons, and blockmasons can be eliminated. Roofers, painters, and drywall and ceiling tile installers could be eliminated when automated machines are introduced for those occupations.

Occupations related to heating, air-conditioning, structural iron, sheet metal, plumbing, carpentry, and electrician may not be able to be replaced by automation. These fields are so specialized that it would take a longer time frame to develop the machines to replicate the jobs.

Operating engineers and other construction equipment operators would rise to a higher profile. As automated machines replace the specialized fields, the role of the operating engineer would evolve to oversee one or more automated machines. Human workers will be needed to monitor and repair the machines. Given the number of machines that could be used for every specialized field, there can be several operating engineers who specialize in the specific machine's function and purpose. Of course, it is possible that one operating engineer may oversee and repair more than one automated machine.

The role of first-line supervisors will likely change from supervising people to managing machines. With the elimination of construction laborers and other workers, the number of first-line supervisors could be reduced. However, if the role of the operating engineer also changes to overseeing machines, there could be a duplication of managerial work. The first-line supervisor and the operating engineer could be merged into one occupation.

Alternatively, the first-line supervisor can still supervise people. But instead of supervising construction workers, the first-line supervisor would supervise operating engineers.

Based on an analysis of a sample of 2019 employment data from the Bureau of Labor Statistics, one-fifth of human workers (20.5 percent) in the construction sector would be displaced by business automation brought on by future technological systems. By contrast, more than double the number of human workers (43.3 percent) would be unaffected by the new systems.

The following 13 occupations would be unaffected by future technological systems:

1. Carpenters (SOC Code: 47–2031)
2. Electricians (SOC Code: 47–2111)
3. First-Line Supervisors of Construction Trades and Extraction Workers (SOC Code: 47–1011)
4. Plumbers, Pipefitters, and Steamfitters (SOC Code: 47–2152)
5. Operating Engineers and Other Construction Equipment Operators (SOC Code: 47–2073)
6. Heating, Air Conditioning, and Refrigeration Mechanics and Installers (SOC Code: 49–9021)
7. Construction Managers (SOC Code: 11–9021)
8. Cost Estimators (SOC Code: 13–1051)
9. Sheet Metal Workers (SOC Code: 47–2211)
10. Helpers – Electricians (SOC Code: 47–3013)
11. Structural Iron and Steel Workers (SOC Code: 47–2221)
12. Project Management Specialists and Business Operations Specialists, All Other (SOC Code: 13–1198)
13. Helpers – Pipelayers, Plumbers, Pipefitters, and Steamfitters (SOC Code: 47–3015)

On the other hand, the following six occupations would be affected by future technological systems:

1. Construction Laborers (SOC Code: 47–2061)
2. Painters, Construction and Maintenance (SOC Code: 47–2141)
3. Cement Masons and Concrete Finishers (SOC Code: 47–2051)
4. Roofers (SOC Code: 47–2181)
5. Drywall and Ceiling Tile Installers (SOC Code: 47–2081)
6. Brickmasons and Blockmasons (SOC Code: 47–2021)

Notes

1 U.S. Bureau of Labor Statistics (2019) "Occupational Employment Statistics (OES) Survey," May 2019 OES Estimates, *U.S. Department of Labor, Bureau of Labor Statistics.*
2 Marco Ceccarelli (2020) "Design and Reconstruction of an Ancient Roman Crane," 8 December, *Advances in Historical Studies*, 9.

3 Ceccarelli, pp. 279, 282.
4 Mining Foundation of the Southwest, "William Smith Otis: 2012 Inductee from Mining's Past," *Mining Foundation of the Southwest.* <www.miningfoundationsw. org/William_Otis>; McCaslin (2018) "William Otis: Grandfather of the Hydraulic Excavator," 24 May, *Texas Final Drive.* <https://info.texasfinaldrive.com/shop-talk-blog/william-otis-grandfather-of-the-hydraulic-excavator>
5 Armstrong Siddeley Heritage Trust (2019) "A Brief History of W. G. Armstrong," *Armstrong Siddeley Heritage Trust.* <www.armstrongsiddeleyheritagetrust.com/ armstrong-master> Encyclopaedia Britannica, "William George Armstrong, Baron Armstrong," *Encyclopaedia Britannica.* <www.britannica.com/ biography/William-George-Armstrong-Baron-Armstrong-of-Cragside>
6 Miroslaw J. Skibniewski (1992) "Current Status of Construction Automation and Robotics in the United States of America," The 9th International Symposium on Automation and Robotics in Construction, 3–5 June 1992.
7 Lauri Koskela (1992) "Process Improvement and Automation in Construction: Opposing or Complementing Approaches?" The 9th International Symposium on Automation and Robotics in Construction, 3–5 June 1992.
8 Yukio Hasegawa (2000) "A New Wave of Construction Automation and Robotics in Japan," 2000 Proceedings of the 17th International Symposium on Automation and Robotics in Construction.
9 Skibniewski.
10 Michael Abrams (2017) "6 Paths to the Automated Construction Site," 8 November, *American Society of Mechanical Engineers.* <www.asme.org/ topics-resources/content/6-paths-automated-construction-site>
11 Martin Fischer and Oussama Khatib (2019) "Leveraging Human-Robot Collaboration in Construction," Summary for CIFE Seed Proposals for Academic Year 2019–20, *Stanford University, Center for Integrated Facility Engineering.* <https://cife.stanford.edu/Seed2019%20 HumanRobotCollaboration>

Chapter 6

Automation in Transportation and Warehousing

6.1 Chapter Summary

Chapter 6 describes the transportation and warehousing industry sector and the demand for human workers in this sector. An historical overview of technological systems in the past is provided. This background of past systems transitions to a review of future technological systems. Based on what has been developed, I predict which future systems would be available in the near and distant future. The chapter concludes with occupations that would be affected and unaffected by business automation brought on by the technological systems designed for transportation and warehousing.

6.2 Description of the Industry

The transportation and warehousing industry sector covers organizations that provide services to transport people and goods across land, rail, sea, and air. Certain businesses may convey crude oil, natural gas, and other substances through a pipeline. Other businesses may store goods in warehouses. According to the North American Industry Classification System, organizations in this sector "provide transportation of passengers and cargo, warehousing and storage for goods, scenic and sightseeing transportation, and support activities related to modes of transportation."[1] This industry sector would have organizations that run the gamut from tourism to commuting to industrial purposes.

DOI: 10.4324/9781003189329-7

All organizations in this sector would need to be registered with state and local authorities. Transportation activities carry high liability as the risk of an accident that causes injury or damage to life or property is high. State and federal governments would be involved to regulate transportation activities. With the liability concern, regulatory requirements, and maintenance and acquisition of a fleet of vehicles, the cost to maintain business operations can be high.

6.3 Demand for Human Workers

In 2019, the transportation and warehousing sector employed an estimated 6.28 million people across the United States, filling 376 occupations that included the full range of vehicle and vessel operators and the support staff to operate transportation and warehouse facilities.[2] Among the top 25 occupations, tractor-trailer truck drivers made up the largest occupation at more than 1 million people – 17 percent of total sector employment. The second and third largest occupations had 873,320 freight and stock movers and 339,640 postal service mail carriers, respectively. Other in-demand occupations included industrial truck operators, light truck drivers, passenger vehicle drivers, flight attendants, stockers and order fillers, mail sorters, and first-line supervisors. Ranked in order of estimated total sector employment, the top 25 occupations were:

1. Heavy and Tractor-Trailer Truck Drivers (SOC Code: 53–3032)
2. Laborers and Freight, Stock, and Material Movers, Hand (SOC Code: 53–7062)
3. Postal Service Mail Carriers (SOC Code: 43–5052)
4. Light Truck Drivers (SOC Code: 53–3033)
5. Passenger Vehicle Drivers, Except Bus Drivers, Transit and Intercity (SOC Code: 53–3058)
6. Industrial Truck and Tractor Operators (SOC Code: 53–7051)
7. Stockers and Order Fillers (SOC Code: 53–7065)
8. First-Line Supervisors of Transportation and Material Moving Workers, Except Aircraft Cargo Handling Supervisors (SOC Code: 53–1047)
9. Flight Attendants (SOC Code: 53–2031)
10. Postal Service Mail Sorters, Processors, and Processing Machine Operators (SOC Code: 43–5053)
11. Customer Service Representatives (SOC Code: 43–4051)

12. Shipping, Receiving, and Inventory Clerks (SOC Code: 43–5071)
13. Office Clerks, General (SOC Code: 43–9061)
14. Dispatchers, Except Police, Fire, and Ambulance (SOC Code: 43–5032)
15. Cargo and Freight Agents (SOC Code: 43–5011)
16. Reservation and Transportation Ticket Agents and Travel Clerks (SOC Code: 43–4181)
17. Bus and Truck Mechanics and Diesel Engine Specialists (SOC Code: 49–3031)
18. Aircraft Mechanics and Service Technicians (SOC Code: 49–3011)
19. Postal Service Clerks (SOC Code: 43–5051)
20. Bus Drivers, Transit and Intercity (SOC Code: 53–3052)
21. Airline Pilots, Copilots, and Flight Engineers (SOC Code: 53–2011)
22. First-Line Supervisors of Office and Administrative Support Workers (SOC Code: 43–1011)
23. General and Operations Managers (SOC Code: 11–1021)
24. Packers and Packagers, Hand (SOC Code: 53–7064)
25. Maintenance and Repair Workers, General (SOC Code: 49–9071)

Of the 376 occupations, 244 occupations were common among six or more industry sectors, making up more than 5 million (80 percent) of total sector employment. These common occupations are important to note. In the event of a mass layoff, people hired in the 244 occupations could take their knowledge and skills and apply them in another industry sector. For example, passenger vehicle drivers, if they were no longer able to transport people in this sector, could move to the educational services sector, the health care sector, or another industry and continue to transport people in the new sector. The top seven common occupations were among the top 25 occupations. Other common occupations included customer service representatives, shipping and receiving clerks, dispatchers, bus drivers and mechanics, and aircraft mechanics.

Unique occupations in this sector highlight the U.S. Postal Service. Ranked in order of most workers in 2019, the Postal Service's occupations included (1) mail carriers, (2) mail sorters and processors, (3) clerks, and (4) postmasters and superintendents. The only large group of workers outside the Postal Service was made up of railroad conductors and yardmasters. Total number of workers who had unique occupations amounted to more than half a million with the majority employed at the U.S. Postal Service.

6.4 Technological Systems in the Past

Vessels – small and large – had evolved in shape, size, and propulsion from prehistoric times to the modern era. The Pesse Canoe, which is dated to around 8000 BCE, was made by carving out the interior of a scotch pine log with a stone axe.[3] Dugout canoes were small watercrafts limited to carrying a few persons and small loads. Another type of watercraft was made of bundled reeds from papyrus (available in Africa), totora (available in South America), or tule (available in North America), depending on where the locals inhabited. With an abundance of available reeds, a reed boat can be larger than a canoe, making it capable of carrying more people and heavier loads than a canoe. A reed or fabric sail and steering oars were fitted on a large reed boat. Most vessels were made of wood by builders who developed their skills and honed their craft across years of practice. Shipbuilding became a trade made up of skilled craftsmen. As new technologies were introduced over decades and centuries, vessels would be improved especially in the area of propulsion. The propulsion system changed from a single sail and oars to multiple sails to a steam-powered paddlewheel to a steam-powered turbine engine to a gas or diesel engine and finally to a nuclear reactor, allowing a vessel to travel from a short distance along a river to a far longer distance across an ocean. The material also changed from reeds to wood to iron and steel and to fiberglass.

Land vehicles also had evolved over time. Before the advent of the wheel, a sledge (or sled) designed with skids was the mode of transportation. A sled continues to be used in arctic regions. Pulled by oxen, dogs, or other animals, the sledge had limited capacity to carry a few persons and small loads. With the use of the wheel, a wide range of carriages in shape, size, and design were made (various names came about such as chariot, cart, coach, stagecoach, and wagon). Some were small and light with a single two-wheel axle. Others had two axles and four wheels, with some models having the front wheels smaller than the rear wheels. Some were as plain and boxy to carry the maximum possible load or as ornate and curvy for use on special occasions and by the upper class. These carriages were pulled by horses or other draft animals. The animal-powered carriages were limited to carry a few persons and small to medium loads.

The steam engine took people and goods off of trails and onto iron tracks. With more power available in a steam engine, a steam-powered locomotive pulled a number of rail cars to carry numerous people and an assortment of heavy and light goods. The propulsion system of the locomotive changed over time to use a diesel engine, diesel-electric, and full electrical power.

The movement of people and goods returned to solid ground with the mass production of the automobile. Powered by the internal combustion engine and built with four wheels, the automobile was unconstrained by tracks and was free to go anywhere the driver would wish. Specialized gas- and diesel-powered vehicles such as tractors and trucks were designed to aid various industries in carrying heavy and very heavy loads.

For more than a 100 years now, technology was developed to carry people and goods across the sky. The propulsion system of an aircraft changed over the decades from a propeller engine to a turboprop engine to a gas turbine (jet engine) and to a turbofan engine (an advanced version of the gas turbine). Depending on the type of engine and the number of engines, a wide range of airplanes were produced for short, medium, and long distances and to carry passengers, cargo, or both passengers and cargo. From an earlier twin propeller engine aircraft that transported 20 passengers to a modern four-engine jet airplane that can transport more than 500 passengers, travel by air has reduced the time to get from point A to point B in a matter of hours as opposed to driving the same distance by automobile or taking another route across the ocean by vessel.

In addition to moving people from one city to another city, innovation had been made to move people faster between floors inside a building. Charles D. Seeberger coined the term, "escalator," after he purchased the patent of a moving stairs design from George Wheeler in 1898.[4] Jesse Reno and Nathan Ames also patented designs of a moving stairs system in 1892 and 1859, respectively. The Otis Elevator Company, founded by Elisha Otis, bought out Reno's company and began installing escalators mainly in department stores in the early 20th century. Earlier in the second half of the 19th century, Elisha Otis had been manufacturing and installing his safety-enhanced elevator designed to move people and goods straight up or down. His elevator was equipped with a safety brake in the event the lifting chain or rope broke.

Public safety had increasingly been a concern with the increase of automobiles and trucks on highways and freeways. To mitigate traffic risk and ensure that roads remained safe and a little less hectic, some innovations had been made such as: a loop detector sensor device installed in street pavement to detect the presence of an automobile (commonly found at street intersections); a ramp meter installed on a freeway on-ramp to control traffic flow onto the freeway; an electronic traffic sign that dynamically changes information whenever necessary to inform drivers about road conditions and other matters of public concern; and the global positioning system (GPS), which comprises a network of satellites to transmit time and precise location data to GPS receivers, aids drivers in accurate navigation and supports transit agencies to track on-time performance of bus and rail services.[5] Of course, the deployment of the automatic traffic signal at street intersections cannot be forgotten. Prior to the traffic signal, a police officer stood in the center of the intersection to direct traffic, stopping vehicles from one direction and allowing vehicles from another direction to pass safely.

6.5 Technological Systems in the Future

Chapter 4 provides descriptions of new technologies related to warehouse operations. To summarize here: a combination of automatic guided vehicles, autonomous mobile robots, and automatic palletizers would improve productivity and efficiency inside the warehouse. Autonomous machines can be programmed to move goods from shelves, load and wrap packaged goods on pallets, and move the palletized goods to the inside of trucks.

Chapter 4 also provides a description of autonomous trucks. The technology implemented in heavy construction equipment can be compared against the technology being used in personal vehicles. Computer software and sensors are the major components that create the system to drive autonomous cars. Remote-control operation is the key difference in the autonomous trucks manufactured by Caterpillar and Komatsu. A human operator is located in an office to monitor the autonomous truck and control how it performs. Remote-control operation and a computer-based system are two approaches to solving the same problem.

The Society of Automotive Engineers International (SAE), a non-profit organization, has established a standard for assessing the level of automation in automotive vehicles. The U.S. Department of Transportation has adopted this standard. According to the SAE, the level of automation can fall along a scale from 0 to 5, where 0 represents "no automation," 1 represents "driver assistance," 2 represents "partial automation," 3 represents "conditional automation," 4 represents "high automation," and 5 represents "full automation." The levels are explained as follows[6]:

Level 0 means that the human driver has full and complete control of the vehicle. Nothing has been automated.

Level 1 means that one function (typically, steering or speed) has been configured to provide assistance to the driver, but the human driver still has full control on all other functions to drive the vehicle.

Level 2 means that two or more functions (typically, steering and speed) have been configured to provide assistance to the driver, but the human driver still remains in full control of all other functions to drive the vehicle.

Level 3 means that all functions have been configured to drive the vehicle, but the human driver must be present to take control of the vehicle whenever the system sends an alert or some other request.

Level 4 means that all functions have been configured to drive the vehicle under certain road and environmental conditions, and the human driver does not need to respond to a system request to take control of the vehicle.

Level 5 means that all functions have been configured to drive the vehicle under all road and environmental conditions. The human driver may not be required to respond to a system request to take control of the vehicle.

A computer-based system designed to control an autonomous vehicle comprises a camera, a light detection and ranging sensor (LIDAR), a radio detection and ranging sensor (RADAR), an infrared sensor, an ultrasonic sensor, a GPS receiver, a collection of digital prebuilt maps, an inertia navigation system comprising a gyroscope and an accelerometer, and a vehicle-to-everything communication system.[7] All of the systems and devices are collecting data to measure the distance in front of the vehicle, detect surrounding objects, communicate with other vehicles and infrastructure, track the precise location of the vehicle, and capture images of what is in front of the vehicle. A computer software program analyzes all of the collected data to determine how the vehicle should move and at what speed. Computer instructions would be executed to control the mechanical functions of the vehicle (e.g., steering, acceleration, braking, and signaling).

All of the collected data would create a perception of reality that may be different from what a human driver actually sees. Each individual sensor may not be 100 percent accurate and thus could have information that is not completely correct. An individual sensor can have a margin of error. Put all sensors together then and the system could present a distorted view of reality. Such a dissonance between what the system sees and the human sees[8] is a major challenge that manufacturers need to overcome.

Chapter 2 describes the randomness behavior pointed out by Alan Turing. Driving a vehicle is a perfect example of what Turing was saying. A human does more than actually see what is directly in front and to the immediate sides. A human also is judging or rather sensing what another vehicle or a pedestrian may be doing.[9] This is something that currently has not been engineered to accomplish by an electronic sensor. Particular behaviors and idiosyncrasies may be encountered on the road. For example, a car at a stop sign may slowly move forward, slowly move back, and again move forward to try to signal something to another stopped car. A car may not completely stop at a stop sign but sluggishly rolls inch by inch. Behaviors are cultural and understood by those in a particular region where the behaviors are prevalent. Only a person from that region would have learned all the possible behaviors. So put another person unfamiliar with local behaviors and there can be a misinterpretation or worse. An autonomous vehicle is like another person who is not familiar with local behaviors. To overcome this problem, an autonomous vehicle needs to learn the behaviors of a particular culture.

As of March 2018, the State of California authorized 52 companies to test autonomous vehicles on California roads.[10] The technology was no longer restricted to testing facilities but has been allowed to experiment on the open road in California.

An autonomous truck can apply the computer-based system of autonomous driving in one of three scenarios: (1) platooning, (2) self-driving a partial route, or (3) self-driving a full route.[11] According to the Government Accountability Office, no technology developers indicated that they were developing their autonomous trucks to drive the entire route from the point of leaving a warehouse where goods are loaded to the point of reaching a final destination where goods are unloaded. Autonomous trucks are being developed and tested to drive a portion of a route such as from entering a freeway to exiting the freeway. A human driver will take control of the autonomous truck when driving in the local area around the warehouse and destination. In the platooning scenario, two or more autonomous trucks are linked together via wireless communication. The multiple trucks operate in a platoon where the lead truck controls acceleration and braking and all the following trucks only control steering. Spacing between the trucks is maintained automatically via the wireless communication to transmit the latest information to all trucks in the platoon.

The U.S. Department of Transportation has been supporting public transit authorities to adopt autonomous vehicles. The agency had announced federal grants in early 2019 to fund demonstration projects. The following seven demonstration and pilot projects represent what has been supported[12]:

1. A lane-assist technology alerts a bus operator with a visual indicator and by vibrating his seat when the bus drifts outside the lane, and the technology will take control of the steering wheel to move the bus back to the center of the lane. (Minnesota Valley Transit Authority)
2. A collision avoidance system uses cameras to warn a bus operator about a possible collision, and the technology will apply the brakes to stop the bus from colliding with the detected object. (Pierce Transit)
3. Jacksonville Transportation Authority tested three autonomous shuttles manufactured by Navya and EasyMile. (Jacksonville Transportation Authority)
4. Two Navya autonomous shuttles were used in mixed traffic along a two-mile round-trip route in Michigan. (University of Michigan)
5. A Navya autonomous shuttle was used in a mixed traffic and high pedestrian scenario in downtown Las Vegas. (City of Las Vegas)
6. Two EasyMile autonomous shuttles were tested in parking lots and on a road between two parking lots with mixed traffic. (Contra Costa Transportation Authority)
7. An EasyMile autonomous shuttle was tested for performance under snow and ice conditions in a closed facility in Minnesota. (Minnesota DOT)

Automated trains have been developed and tested. Approximately 90 automated metro lines exist in operation around the world.[13] The technology to operate trains without a human has been in place since the late 1960s. The London Underground's Victoria Line started using automation in 1967. The San Francisco Bay Area Rapid Transit (BART) system has had the equipment to run full automation of its trains since the 1970s, but the technology has yet to be used.[14]

Autonomous vessels designed to carry shipping containers are in development.[15] The first electric and autonomous cargo ship had completed its maiden voyage between two Norwegian cities in November 2021.[16] This 80-meter vessel made by a Norwegian company will conduct tests of the technology over the next 2 years.[17] A second autonomous cargo ship developed and funded by a group of Japanese organizations is planned to set sail on a 236-mile trip in early 2022.[18] This Japanese vessel includes remote-control operation in the event that a human needs to take control of operating the vessel.

With technological systems capable of operating vessels and vehicles automatically over sea and land, there is one part in the business process that remains to be automated. As far as shipping and receiving goods go, the supply chain system is a complex network of manufacturers, suppliers, distributors, resellers, and freight carriers. Management of the logistics to move and track packages is a complicated area. Amazon.com managed to create an efficient system. It invested its resources to create an "integrated, start-to-finish [global] supply network" that includes 184 fulfillment centers, 100,000 warehouse robots, 50 airplanes, 7,000 trucks, 20,000 vans for last-mile delivery, 600 retails stores, and 5,300 shipping containers shipped on Amazon-owned vessels.[19] By controlling nearly all aspects of the supply chain, Amazon.com has the capability to process an inventory of 100 million products to deliver packages to customers in two days. This controlled environment gives Amazon.com the advantage to communicate with partners effectively and to resolve supply-chain issues quickly as they arise.

Amazon.com represents an extreme case but illustrates the point of managing the flow of information. Numerous documents such as a customer sales order, a packing list, a bill of laden, and a customs declaration involved in shipping and transporting goods have to be managed and retained. In the last three decades, management information systems have been used to enter and store corporate and supplier data that allow an organization to keep track of vendors, inventory, and financials. The information systems go by various names such as an enterprise resource planning (ERP) system, a transportation management system, and a warehouse management solution.[20] In any case, the information system gives business managers the ability to review the progress of operations with timely information from which they can make evidence-based decisions.

Information technology providers have advanced development of an information system to include business intelligence and cloud-based operation. In the past, systems had operated in a traditional client-server environment where corporate employees accessed the system within a private computer network in a building. Partners would be given a different type of account and a rather cumbersome way to access the corporate system. Today, employees and partners can access the information system via the Internet from wherever they may be located.

The second advancement in the information system is business intelligence. The computer software is programmed to analyze corporate and supplier data stored in the system. As a result of processing the data, charts would be generated from the software program and displayed to the business manager. The business manager can then review the results and make a decision. Instead of having a human to read and analyze numerous records, the information system can do the analysis more efficiently. All the business manager can essentially do is log in to the system and view the reports.

The last technological system to include relates to safety designed to prevent train-to-train collisions, train derailments, train movements onto wrong tracks, and unauthorized train movements. The Rail Safety Improvement Act of 2008 requires the implementation of a positive train control (PTC) system on certain railroad lines whose trains carry passengers and hazardous materials. The law further requires the PTC system to have interoperability so that various locomotives operated by different companies can communicate with each other. The PTC system comprises an on-board computer system in the locomotive, numerous wayside systems and base-station radios situated at various points along the track, and an information system.[21] All of the electronic systems communicate via a wireless computer network. The information system stores data related to the current location, direction, and speed of all trains operating on the rail line, the current status of all track signals and switches, and the current status of tracks. The wayside systems monitor track signals and switches and tracks. The on-board computer, which includes a GPS receiver, communicates with a wayside station and the information system, receiving information about current track status and sending the latest information about the locomotive. The train operator can make a decision based on the information received, allowing adequate time to bring the train to a stop. If no action is taken in the event of a warning, the PTC system can instruct the on-board computer to apply the brakes and bring the train to a complete stop automatically.[22]

6.6 Forecasting of Technological Systems

Management information systems, PTC systems, automated trains, and autonomous shuttles are available now. Level 1 and 2 autonomous cars are also available. Autonomous shuttles would be limited to certain driving areas where the risk of an accident with pedestrians and automobiles is low.

Within the next 7 years, autonomous trucks would be limited to particular areas where there is no commuter traffic. Autonomous trucks would operate within defined boundaries of a given space. Autonomous vessels developed by Japan and Norway would be in full operation. Some public buses in a few cities would start using lane-assist technology or a collision avoidance system.

From 8 to 15 years, additional autonomous vessels will be in operation. More autonomous shuttles will be deployed. The concept of platooning will be implemented in a number of states but not nationwide. In 12 years, level 3 autonomous trucks will be able to drive a partial route that is restricted to freeways.

From 16 to 25 years in the future, autonomous vessels from other manufacturers will be in operation, increasing the number of vessels. Autonomous shuttles will be able to operate in suburban and rural areas. Level 5 autonomous cars will be able to drive on public roads, limited to suburban and rural areas. Level 3 autonomous cars can be used in urban areas. Public buses in more cities would be using lane-assist technology or a collision avoidance system. In 20 years, the concept of platooning will be implemented nationwide. Near the end of this time period (24–25 years), level 3 autonomous trucks will be able to drive on public roads.

6.7 Changes in Jobs, Roles, and Occupations

Nine out of the 25 occupations listed above could be significantly impacted by future technological systems. Occupations related to warehousing such as freight and stock movers, order fillers, shipping and receiving, and packing can be eliminated. If automated mobile robots are developed to do the jobs of mail sorters, mail processors, and postal service clerks, then those occupations can be eliminated. If automated mobile robots are developed to do the jobs of flight attendants, ticket agents, and cargo agents, then those occupations can be eliminated as well.

All driving-related occupations plus airline pilots and postal service mail carriers would not be eliminated. But the role of drivers will change to overseeing vehicle operation. In an event that the vehicle needs to stop or otherwise needs to be controlled, the driver must intervene to take control. Drivers would still be needed to do other tasks. Their job responsibilities will shift to new focus areas. Those drivers who carry passengers can focus on helping passengers especially persons with disabilities. Truck drivers would focus on loading and unloading freight.

Mechanics and repair workers will still be needed to service the vehicles. Their job responsibilities would not change. But they will need training on the new technologies in order to repair the autonomous vehicles.

Based on an analysis of a sample of 2019 employment data from the Bureau of Labor Statistics, more than a quarter of all human workers (27.3 percent) in the transportation sector would be displaced by business automation brought on by future technological systems. By contrast, a larger proportion of human workers (44.7 percent) would be unaffected by the new systems. This difference between human workers who would be affected and unaffected is similar to the analysis in the construction sector. The following 11 occupations would be unaffected by future technological systems:

1. Heavy and Tractor-Trailer Truck Drivers (SOC Code: 53–3032)
2. Postal Service Mail Carriers (SOC Code: 43–5052)
3. Light Truck Drivers (SOC Code: 53–3033)
4. Passenger Vehicle Drivers, Except Bus Drivers, Transit and Intercity (SOC Code: 53–3058)
5. Industrial Truck and Tractor Operators (SOC Code: 53–7051)
6. First-Line Supervisors of Transportation and Material Moving Workers, Except Aircraft Cargo Handling Supervisors (SOC Code: 53–1047)
7. Bus and Truck Mechanics and Diesel Engine Specialists (SOC Code: 49–3031)
8. Aircraft Mechanics and Service Technicians (SOC Code: 49–3011)
9. Bus Drivers, Transit and Intercity (SOC Code: 53–3052)
10. Airline Pilots, Copilots, and Flight Engineers (SOC Code: 53–2011)
11. Maintenance and Repair Workers, General (SOC Code: 49–9071)

On the other hand, the following nine occupations would be affected by future technological systems:

1. Laborers and Freight, Stock, and Material Movers, Hand (SOC Code: 53–7062)
2. Stockers and Order Fillers (SOC Code: 53–7065)
3. Flight Attendants (SOC Code: 53–2031)
4. Postal Service Mail Sorters, Processors, and Processing Machine Operators (SOC Code: 43–5053)
5. Shipping, Receiving, and Inventory Clerks (SOC Code: 43–5071)
6. Cargo and Freight Agents (SOC Code: 43–5011)
7. Reservation and Transportation Ticket Agents and Travel Clerks (SOC Code: 43–4181)
8. Postal Service Clerks (SOC Code: 43–5051)
9. Packers and Packagers, Hand (SOC Code: 53–7064)

Notes

1 U.S. Bureau of Labor Statistics (2021) "Industries at a Glance: Transportation and Warehousing: NAICS 48–49," 8 January, *U.S. Department of Labor, Bureau of Labor Statistics*. <www.bls.gov/iag/tgs/iag48-49.htm>

2 U.S. Bureau of Labor Statistics (2019) "Occupational Employment Statistics (OES) Survey," May 2019 OES Estimates, *U.S. Department of Labor, Bureau of Labor Statistics*.

3 Geoffrey Migiro (2018) "The Oldest Ships in the World," 21 May, *WorldAtlas* <www.worldatlas.com/articles/the-oldest-ships-in-the-world.html> Drents Museum (2016) "The Pesse Canoe," *Drents Museum*. <https://drentsmuseum.nl/en/in-the-spotlight-top-exhibits/pesse-canoe>

4 Matt Blitz (2016) "Movin' on Up: The Curious Birth and Rapid Rise of the Escalator," 6 April, *Popular Mechanics*. <www.popularmechanics.com/technology/gadgets/a20291/moving-on-up-the-escalato>

5 Ashley Auer, Shelley Feese, and Stephen Lockwood (2016) "History of Intelligent Transportation Systems," Report produced by Booz Allen Hamilton, FHWA-JPO-16-329, May 2016, *U.S. Department of Transportation, Intelligent Transportation Systems Joint Program Office*, pp. 4–5.

6 U.S. Government Accountability Office (2019) "Automated Trucking: Federal Agencies Should Take Additional Steps to Prepare for Potential Workforce Effects," Report to the Subcommittee on Transportation, Housing and Urban Development, and Related Agencies, Committee on Appropriations, U.S. Senate, GAO-19-161, March 2019. *U.S. Government Accountability Office*, pp. 8–10; Ranjit Godavarthy (2019) "Transit Automation Technologies: A Review of Transit Agency Perspective," Report produced by North Dakota State University, Upper Great Plains Transportation Institute, Small Urban and Rural Transit Center, December 2019, *U.S. Department of Transportation*, p. 3.

7 U.S. Government Accountability Office (2017) "Automated Vehicles: Comprehensive Plan Could Help DOT Address Challenges," Report to Congressional Committees, GAO-18–132, November 2017, *U.S. Government Accountability Office*, p. 6; GAO, "Automated Trucking," p. 10.

8 P. A. Hancock, Illah Nourbakhsh, and Jack Stewart (2019) "On the Future of Transportation in an Era of Automated and Autonomous Vehicles," 16 April, *PNAS*, 116, no. 16, p. 7687.

9 The GAO recognized and addressed the issue of communicating intent. "Automated Vehicles," pp. 13–15.

10 Hancock, p. 7684.

11 GAO, "Automated Trucking," pp. 11–15.

12 Godavarthy, pp. 4–6.

13 José Viegas (2017) "Automation and the Future of Public Transport," 24 February, *Intelligent Transport*. <www.intelligenttransport.com/transport-articles/72914/automation-future-public-transport/>

14 Wayne D. Cottrell (2015) "A Very Brief History of Automation in Transportation," 6 October, *ATRA*.

15 Michael Daher et al. (2019) "How Are Global Shippers Evolving to Meet Tomorrow's Demand? The Future of the Movement of Goods," *Deloitte Insights*, p. 8.

16 Ameya Paleja (2021) "World's First Autonomous Electric Container Ship Completed Its First Trip: And It Will Save 1,000 Tons of Carbon Emissions a Year," 22 November, *Interesting Engineering*; Victoria Klesty (2021) "Yara Debuts World's First Autonomous Electric Container Ship," 19 November, *Reuters*.

17 Yara International (2021) "Yara to Start Operating the World's First Fully Emission-free Container Ship," Corporate Press Release, 19 November, *Yara International*. <www.yara.com/corporate-releases/yara-to-start-operating-the-worlds-first-fully-emission-free-container-ship/>

18 River Davis and Tsuyoshi Inajima (2021) "First Autonomous Cargo Ship Faces Test With 236-Mile Voyage," 30 August, *Bloomberg*; Lawrence Hodge (2021) "Two Autonomous Cargo Ships Are about to Set Sail," 1 September, *Jalopnik*.

19 Daher, pp. 4–5.

20 Daher, p. 7.

21 Association of American Railroads (2020) "Freight Railroads and Positive Train Control (PTC)," Fact Sheet, August 2020. <www.aar.org/wp-content/uploads/2020/08/AAR-PTC-Fact-Sheet.pdf>.

22 Union Pacific. "Positive Train Control." <www.up.com/media/media_kit/ptc/about-ptc/>.

Chapter 7

Automation in Accommodation and Food Services

7.1 Chapter Summary

Chapter 7 describes the accommodation and food services industry sector and the demand for human workers in this sector. An historical overview of technological systems in the past is provided. This background of past systems transitions to a review of future technological systems. Based on what has been developed, I predict which future systems would be available in the near and distant future. The chapter concludes with occupations that would be affected and unaffected by business automation brought on by the technological systems designed for accommodation and food services.

7.2 Description of the Industry

The accommodation and food services industry sector covers businesses that provide lodging service, meal and beverage service, or both lodging and meal service to people for immediate consumption.[1] Businesses in this sector would be hotels, motels, restaurants, and fast-food restaurants. Accommodation businesses would cater primarily to persons who are not residents of a given city or town. Restaurants would cater to anyone, non-resident and resident alike. Hospitality is central to the success of this sector,

DOI: 10.4324/9781003189329-8

as businesses operate to provide basic necessities to customers especially to strangers who have come from a distant place.

Many restaurants and small-scale motels would be small businesses operated by an individual, a family, or a franchise operated in partnership with an established corporation. Large-scale hotels would be operated by a corporation.

Operating lodging and food service establishments has been needed as long as people needed to find some rest from a long day of travel. The Nisiyama Onsen Keiunkan has operated in Japan since AD 705.[2] This hot springs resort is listed as the oldest hotel in the Guinness World Records.[3] In the late 1700s and early 1800s in the United States, inns and taverns sprang up to offer a basic room and some food for travelers who needed to spend the night.[4] Most inns were informal establishments. The idea of a hotel would emerge in Europe in the 18th century[5] and in the United States in the early 19th century[6] to formalize the experience of serving travelers. Individual rooms with their own bathroom and a secured door for privacy would be developed. Luxurious features such as decorated ceilings and crystal chandeliers would be added in some hotels. Hotel services and features would improve into the 20th century where a greater number of people would be able to travel more frequently as a result of the use of the automobile and the aircraft.

7.3 Demand for Human Workers

In 2019, the accommodation and food services sector employed an estimated 14.07 million people across the United States, filling 273 occupations.[7] This industry sector employed the second highest number of people among the eight industry sectors studied in this book. Among the top 25 occupations, fast food workers made up the largest occupation at 3.38 million people. The second and third largest occupations had 2.39 million waiters and waitresses and 1.33 million restaurant cooks, respectively. These top 3 occupations made up half of total sector employment. Other in-demand occupations included bartenders, fast food cooks, food preparation workers, dishwashers, housekeeping cleaners, hosts and hostesses, desk clerks, cashiers, and first-line supervisors. Ranked in order of estimated total sector employment, the top 25 occupations were:

1. Fast Food and Counter Workers (SOC Code: 35–3023)
2. Waiters and Waitresses (SOC Code: 35–3031)
3. Cooks, Restaurant (SOC Code: 35–2014)

4. First-Line Supervisors of Food Preparation and Serving Workers (SOC Code: 35–1012)
5. Bartenders (SOC Code: 35–3011)
6. Cooks, Fast Food (SOC Code: 35–2011)
7. Food Preparation Workers (SOC Code: 35–2021)
8. Maids and Housekeeping Cleaners (SOC Code: 37–2012)
9. Dishwashers (SOC Code: 35–9021)
10. Hosts and Hostesses, Restaurant, Lounge, and Coffee Shop (SOC Code: 35–9031)
11. Dining Room and Cafeteria Attendants and Bartender Helpers (SOC Code: 35–9011)
12. Cashiers (SOC Code: 41–2011)
13. Hotel, Motel, and Resort Desk Clerks (SOC Code: 43–4081)
14. Driver/Sales Workers (SOC Code: 53–3031)
15. Food Service Managers (SOC Code: 11–9051)
16. Maintenance and Repair Workers, General (SOC Code: 49–9071)
17. Cooks, Short Order (SOC Code: 35–2015)
18. General and Operations Managers (SOC Code: 11–1021)
19. Chefs and Head Cooks (SOC Code: 35–1011)
20. Janitors and Cleaners, Except Maids and Housekeeping Cleaners (SOC Code: 37–2011)
21. Food Servers, Non-restaurant (SOC Code: 35–3041)
22. Cooks, Institution and Cafeteria (SOC Code: 35–2012)
23. Security Guards (SOC Code: 33–9032)
24. Gambling Dealers (SOC Code: 39–3011)
25. Food Preparation and Serving Related Workers, All Other (SOC Code: 35–9099)

Of the 273 occupations, three-quarters of the occupations were common among six or more industry sectors, making up 94 percent of total sector employment at 13.27 million people. These common occupations are important to note. In the event of a mass layoff, people hired in the 204 occupations could take their knowledge and skills and apply them in another industry sector. For example, fast food and counter workers, if they found themselves unemployed, could move to the educational services sector, the health care sector, or another industry where they can serve meals to people. The top 22 common occupations were among the top 25 occupations. Other common occupations included light truck drivers, laundry workers, food preparation workers, accounting clerks, office clerks, sales representatives, and customer service representatives.

7.4 Technological Systems in the Past

The process of managing and issuing guest keys has improved from the days when keys were used. For most of the period in which hotels existed, guests had to use a physical key to access their room. Some hotels and smaller establishments would have maintained one master set of all room keys – like keeping all keys on a large ring at the front desk.[8] Guests would have to see the proprietor every time they needed to get into their room. Other hotels would have issued a key to a guest who would be able to keep it on hand during her stay, eliminating the need to see the proprietor every time access to the room was needed.

The technology behind the key had to have a level of security so that the bolt securing a door to the wall can be prevented from moving. In 1778, Robert Barron designed a tumbler lock that required an inserted key to lift a number of tumblers (later called, levers) to a certain height in order to free the bolt from its locked position.[9] Adding more levers and configuring varied heights that the levers can move to increase the level of security in the lock. Barron's lock replaced the warded lock (or ward lock) that had been in use since the 10th century.

In 1784 and 1798, Joseph Bramah designed and improved his lock by first using 18 iron slides with one spring and then using 13 steel slides with each slide having its own spring.[10] His key design was cylindrical that when inserted in the lock depressed the slides a certain depth.[11] Each lock had the slides set to varied depths, creating a unique lock for a door.

In 1861, Linus Yale, Jr. designed a tumbler lock that required a grooved cylindrical key to push down a number of pistons and drivers (as Yale called them) into their pin chambers, which caused the bolt (the tumbler) to be movable.[12] When the key was turned, the bolt revolved to its unlocked position. The bolt returned to its locked (unmovable) position when the key was removed. A spring inside each pin chamber allowed the piston and driver to be forced down by the insertion of the key. All of the drivers were forced down to the same level to cause the bolt to be free. Varied lengths of the pistons and drivers required a unique key whose groove had to be carved in a particular way so as to make the drivers align when fully pressed.

Yale's original lock design would be later modified to use a flat key with a serrated edge – much like a key used today. The principle of unlocking the bolt would not have changed.

Early inns and taverns would likely have used a warded lock. Early hotels and other establishments would have used Barron's or Bramah's lock design. Hotels in the 20th century would have used Yale's lock design.

In 1979, Tor Sornes designed a lock that required a key card to form a completed matrix of punched holes with a code card situated in the locking device.[13] A correct key card with juxtaposed punched holes allowed balls and blocking pins to be aligned, the alignment of which caused the locking mechanism to be movable. An incorrect key card would not align the balls and blocking pins and therefore would keep the locking mechanism in its locked position. A spring was used to move the ball and blocking pin up or down. When the correct key card was inserted into the slot, a person can turn the doorknob to unlock and open the door. Removal of the key card returned the balls and blocking pins to their original positions, putting the locking mechanism in its locked position. The key card and code card were made to have varied combinations of punched holes, creating a unique lock for a door.

Sornes' design created an inexpensive system to change locks and issue new key cards. Both the key card and code card were made of plastic or cardboard. And they were easily punched with the necessary holes. If a key card was lost, a new key card and code card can be quickly replaced with a different set of punched holes. The new pair of cards would cause the lost key card to be invalid. In contrast to a conventional Yale lock, the entire key and lock system designed by Yale would have to be replaced. In Sornes' design, just the key card and code card would be replaced – not the entire system.

Predating Sornes in 1975, Walter Fromm designed a lock that required a magnetic stripe card (or magstripe card) to match a certain code in an electronic locking device, which used an electromagnet to release a locking armature thus causing the locking mechanism to move freely.[14] Fromm's design used an electronic circuit configured with a controller to read the data stored on the magstripe card. The magstripe card was inserted into a slot. If the magstripe card did not match the code, the locking armature remained in place and the locking mechanism remained in the locked position. A small colored LED light may be a part of the circuit to indicate whether the code matched.

In Fromm's lock design, the key is the magnetic stripe card, which would be encoded with a room number and the dates that a guest can use the room. The magstripe card can be quickly written and re-written with new information. Hotels and other establishments would likely have used this design or another type that used a magnetic stripe card from the 1980s to now. An alternative electronic locking device different from the Fromm design may have been developed but still used the magnetic stripe card as the key.

The process of preparing and delivering food and beverages for immediate consumption has had at least four different systems or methods. The automat, first opened in Berlin, Germany in 1895 and then in Philadelphia, Pennsylvania in 1902, offered ready-to-eat hot or cold meals via a wall-size vending machine. It would open in other European cities and in several locations in New York. In the United States, a person would walk up to a wall of windows, browse the selection of dishes, pick one, drop a number of nickels in the slot, turn a knob for the glass door to click open, lift the door, and pull out the dish.[15] Hot coffee was also available. It all looked convenient and easy from the customer's view. However, the operator of the automat still needed to hire cooks, dishwashers, and support staff to replenish all the compartments with food.[16] Hired workers were in the back completely hidden from all customers.

A vending machine was a self-enclosed mechanical system designed for a person to pay for a product, select a product from one or more options, and receive the product from a dispenser outlet. A person can receive his selected product in a few seconds. Depending on what type of product was to be dispensed, the configuration of the machinery was different. A soft drink vending machine, for example, included a refrigeration unit to dispense chilled soda. A coffee vending machine included a heating unit to heat water to a specified temperature. A snack vending machine included numerous metal spiral holders, each one of which was used to hold a single group of a snack product (e.g., a brand of potato chips). All vending machines included a coin receptor to check the difference between a quarter, a dime, a nickel, and other coins and to drop the coin in the corresponding coin receptacle; a selection panel composed of buttons that corresponded to products (snacks or drinks); a dispenser outlet or tray to receive the product; and an outlet to receive a rejected coin. The coin receptor was designed to detect and reject a slug. This description of a vending machine would have been used as early as the late 1950s.

Earlier vending machines in the United States mostly dispensed a single product and accepted one kind of coin denomination. Chewing gum machines came into existence in 1888 followed by gumball machines in 1907. Carbonated soda machines were manufactured and distributed in the 1920s and 1930s. Earlier soda machines mixed carbonated water and flavored syrup and dispensed the drink into a paper cup. The completed mix in bottles came shortly after paper cups.

Vending machines starting from the late 1950s and over the next decades would evolve in sophistication and variety, offering more product selections and improved convenience. Cold-cut sandwiches and pre-cooked hamburgers would later become available. Dollar bills of various denominations would be accepted in later machines. Electronics would be incorporated into the design to process and display the customer's selection and to calculate and disburse any change that would be due.

The ubiquity of the vending machine is attributed to its design and portability. All the necessary parts to deliver a food or beverage were contained within a single machine that can be transported. Several vending machines were hauled on a light industrial truck to any building or location for installation. Once installed, the vending machine operated 24 hours a day without a human operator. Periodically or on call, a mechanic came in to service the machine and replenish it with new products. But this human worker did not need to be present at all hours of the day.

The vending machine eliminated the requirement to prepare and cook food on-site. All of the food products came from a food manufacturer. Potato chips, crackers, candy bars, chewing gum, and later sandwiches and other food products were purchased from suppliers. A mechanic responsible for his group of vending machines was responsible for loading the food products into the machines. And of course, the mechanic removed old food products that had not been selected and consumed for a long time.

Delivering fresh and hot food products in a more convenient way was done through a self-service restaurant or cafeteria. There is some debate on the origin of the cafeteria, but accounts referred to the late 1880s and early 1890s of when the first cafeteria appeared. The cafeteria would grow in popularity in the early 20th century. Driven by the need to serve an increasing number of people who moved to urban cities, the self-service restaurant provided an assortment of food ready to take on a counter. Diners did not have to sit at a table and wait 20 or 30 minutes for their order to be prepared and cooked. A diner can simply browse the counter, take what she wanted, pay a cashier for the selected dish, and sit at a table to eat her meal. The cafeteria concept would become standard practice in schools, hospitals, and public institutions where a significantly large group of people had to be served. Large corporations that employed hundreds of workers would also have implemented a cafeteria in their facilities.

Self-service restaurants that catered to the general population declined by the 1960s. During this time, fast food franchise restaurants grew in popularity. A corporation licensed and supported a network of entrepreneurs to manage and operate a fast food restaurant in their local area. This allowed the corporation to grow rapidly while limiting its risk. Each franchisee took on their share of the risk. In exchange, the franchisee was supplied with specially made food products that can be quickly cooked in a shorter period of time. Periodically on a regular schedule, the fast food restaurant received stocks of ingredients. On any given day, customers would come in, place an order, pay for their order, and wait a few minutes for their order to be completed.

7.5 Technological Systems in the Future

A Chinese company appears to have fully automated the restaurant dining experience. In its restaurant, a diner makes his selections with a robotic waiter, goes to his seat at a table, waits for a robotic cook to prepare his order, and receives his completed order automatically either from a rail system or from a tray carried by a mobile robot. Among the 40 robotic cooks capable of cooking 200 dishes, a noodle-making machine can complete 120 bowls of noodles in an hour.[17]

The Chinese restaurant example shows three areas that are being automated: (1) ordering a meal, (2) cooking a meal, and (3) receiving a meal. A fully automated restaurant would need all three areas automated.

Three different technological systems have been developed to place an order. A kiosk system comprised a computer, a touch-screen display screen, and a network connection allows a person to browse a menu and select menu choices by touching the screen. A payment terminal may be connected to the kiosk to accept payment via credit card. The selected order is transmitted to another computer where restaurant staff can view the new order and follow through on completing the order.

A tabletop system comprised of a tablet computer, a specialized software program, a payment system, and a wireless network connection sits on an individual table where a diner can place an order after being seated. Instead of reading a laminated menu brochure, the diner can browse an electronic menu, select menu choices, and pay for the order by touching the screen on the tabletop system. The system may have a magnetic stripe reader, a chip reader, or a near field communication (NFC) reader for the diner to make a payment. In the case of the NFC reader, the diner can use her smartphone to make a payment. The selected order is transmitted to another computer where restaurant staff can view the new order and follow through on completing the order.

A Web site with an e-commerce system is the third way of ordering. Before entering the restaurant, a person can visit the Web site, browse an electronic menu, select menu choices, and pay for the order by credit card, and receive a receipt. The selected order is transmitted to a computer where restaurant staff can view the order and follow through on completing the order. The person then goes to the restaurant to pick up his order. By the time he arrives, the order would be ready.

If a person is already in the restaurant, he could connect to the Web site and e-commerce system via a QR code and proceed to place an order. This alternative method enables the person to order from a smartphone.

The submitted order gets processed by a collaborative robot or co-bot. A co-bot would be a robotic arm comprised of a computer, servo-motors, and sensors. An advanced co-bot is programmed with machine learning to learn the cooking trade and adapt to techniques and mistakes. The co-bot would not necessarily replace a human cook but would operate alongside the cook. Some example co-bots include a short-order cook that flips and grills, a pizza-maker that spreads tomato sauce and loads and unloads the oven, a sushi chef that makes 3,600 sushi items in an hour, and a dessert chef that delivers seven flavors of frozen yogurt with six different toppings.[18]

A start-up company developed a salad-making machine that is a cross between a co-bot and a vending machine. This is a self-contained machine that can be installed in a location with high traffic of people coming and going. All of the ingredients are kept at a constant temperature.[19] The machine can create a salad from 1,000 different combinations and 22 ingredients in less than 60 seconds.[20]

After the co-bot has completed cooking, the meal is delivered on an autonomous mobile robot. Similar to that described in Chapter 4, an autonomous mobile robot is comprised of a computer, multiple sensors, and a compartment or a tray to hold the food. The mobile robot is programmed to move freely across a restaurant floor.

The process of serving hotel guests is more involved than serving restaurant diners. In a hotel environment, a guest arrives and checks in, receives a room key, gets a porter to carry her luggage, enters her room, and gets settled into her new environment. From time to time, the guest may ask for assistance from the front desk. While the guest is away, her room will be cleaned. Her room as well as all other rooms and the entire building are monitored for physical security and energy usage. At the end of the guest's stay, she checks out.

A self-service kiosk similar to the ordering kiosk described above has been developed to allow a guest to check-in and check-out. A particular hotel may provide a specialized computer software program that a guest installs in her smartphone. This software program can have functions that allow the guest to check-in, check-out, receive an electronic room key, and interact with electronic devices situated in the room.

New key and locking devices have been developed since the magnetic stripe card. A locking device may be equipped with a radio frequency identification (RFID) reader or an NFC reader to enable the door to unlock without touching the door. A guest is issued an RFID tag or an NFC tag and can use the tag to unlock the door. The tag is held up close to the locking device where data can be transferred wirelessly. The locking device is configured to use either RFID or NFC technology and to process the transmitted data.

A guest's smartphone can receive an electronic room key, using a hotel's software program. In this case, the smartphone performs as the NFC tag. The guest holds up her smartphone in front of the locking device and if the data match between the tag and the reader, the door will unlock. If the data do not match, the door will remain locked.

An autonomous mobile robot, similar in function to that described in Chapter 4, has been developed to carry luggage, linens, and room service. This machine performs like a hotel porter. It is programmed to move freely around the hotel to deliver items to a guest room.

Autonomous mobile robots related to cleaning have been developed to vacuum carpets and to scrub tiled floors and other hard surfaces. These automated cleaning machines control and manage the mechanical parts of the cleaning apparatus.

Another type of autonomous mobile robot is designed to perform like a security guard. This security robot is programmed to move freely at a slow speed to monitor the environment. Equipped with cameras, microphones, speakers, and LIDAR, the security robot can detect people in the area, record video, and broadcast pre-recorded and live messages.

Energy consumption can be reduced through a combination of a smart heating, ventilation, and air-conditioning (HVAC) system, sensors, and smart lighting. An LED light has advanced over the years to illuminate a room at equal brightness to that of an incandescent lightbulb. A new type of an LED light comprises an electronic circuit, a wireless network connection, and a software program. By interacting with the controls programmed in the software, a person can change the brightness or change the color of the light.

An occupancy sensor can be installed in a room to turn a light on or off automatically. This type of sensor is a motion sensor. When the occupancy sensor detects motion in the room, the sensor will automatically turn the light on. When the occupancy sensor no longer detects motion, the sensor will automatically turn the light off.

A vacancy sensor can be installed in a room to turn a light off automatically when the room is vacant and motion is no longer detected. With this sensor, the light must be manually turned on.

A humidity sensor can be installed in a room to monitor the level of humidity. When it detects excess humidity, the sensor will automatically turn on a ventilation fan.

Advancements in the design of an HVAC system have been made to integrate an electronic circuit with the mechanical parts of the HVAC system. This creates a smart HVAC system that enables the HVAC to operate at peak, energy-efficient performance. For example, a variable speed compressor unit can be adjusted to run at a lower capacity. A traditional compressor runs at constant speed at full capacity. Energy can be saved by adjusting the speed of the compressor. The embedded electronics in the HVAC system can communicate with the thermostats located throughout the building and make adjustments to cooling and heating.

7.6 Forecasting of Technological Systems

All of the technological systems except for two systems are available now. Smart HVAC systems could become widely available in about 8–15 years from now. Because of the variety of food dishes that can be prepared, numerous collaborative robot cooks specializing in a wide range of meals would need to be developed and tested. Thus, it will take time to deploy robot cooks. Within the next 7 years, there could be a group of robot cooks that can do more complicated cooking beyond hamburgers, salads, and sushi. Collaborative robot cooks may be able to do food preparation by this time. In about 8–15 years, another group of robot cooks could be developed and ready to prepare a wider range of meals.

7.7 Changes in Jobs, Roles, and Occupations

Thirteen out of the 25 occupations (half of the occupations) listed above can be eliminated. Fast food workers, waiters, food preparation workers, dishwashers, restaurant hosts, cashiers, hotel desk clerks, and janitors would be replaced by machines. If machines are developed for bartending, bartenders can be replaced.

Some cooks such as those who prepare fast food and short orders could be eliminated. Other cooks who prepare meals in restaurants, institutions, and cafeterias may still be needed. Chefs and head cooks would likely continue to hold on to their jobs, although their role would change to focus on supervising machines. The responsibilities of chefs could focus on assisting the collaborative robots.

Dining room attendants, first-line supervisors, and food service managers would still be needed. These three occupations might be consolidated into one occupation. Their role would change from supervising people to managing machines.

Maids and housekeepers would still be needed. There are still other tasks such as cleaning the bathroom, making the bed, and laundry for which autonomous mobile robots have not been developed yet. The housekeeper's job will be made easier, as machines assist in lighten the load to keep an entire room clean and in order.

Based on an analysis of a sample of 2019 employment data from the Bureau of Labor Statistics, 61.5 percent of human workers in the accommodation and food services sector would be displaced by business automation brought on by future technological systems. A quarter of all human workers (25.2 percent) in the accommodation and food services sector would be unaffected by the new systems. The following eight occupations would be unaffected by future technological systems:

1. Cooks, Restaurant (SOC Code: 35–2014)
2. First-Line Supervisors of Food Preparation and Serving Workers (SOC Code: 35–1012)
3. Maids and Housekeeping Cleaners (SOC Code: 37–2012)
4. Dining Room and Cafeteria Attendants and Bartender Helpers (SOC Code: 35–9011)
5. Food Service Managers (SOC Code: 11–9051)
6. Maintenance and Repair Workers, General (SOC Code: 49–9071)
7. Chefs and Head Cooks (SOC Code: 35–1011)
8. Cooks, Institution and Cafeteria (SOC Code: 35–2012)

On the other hand, the following 13 occupations would be affected by future technological systems:

1. Fast Food and Counter Workers (SOC Code: 35–3023)
2. Waiters and Waitresses (SOC Code: 35–3031)
3. Bartenders (SOC Code: 35–3011)
4. Food Preparation Workers (SOC Code: 35–2021)
5. Dishwashers (SOC Code: 35–9021)
6. Hosts and Hostesses, Restaurant, Lounge, and Coffee Shop (SOC Code: 35–9031)
7. Cashiers (SOC Code: 41–2011)
8. Hotel, Motel, and Resort Desk Clerks (SOC Code: 43–4081)
9. Janitors and Cleaners, Except Maids and Housekeeping Cleaners (SOC Code: 37–2011)
10. Food Servers, Non-restaurant (SOC Code: 35–3041)
11. Security Guards (SOC Code: 33–9032)
12. Gambling Dealers (SOC Code: 39–3011)
13. Food Preparation and Serving Related Workers, All Other (SOC Code: 35–9099)

Notes

1 U.S. Bureau of Labor Statistics (2021) "Industries at a Glance: Accommodation and Food Services: NAICS 72," 8 January, *U.S. Department of Labor, Bureau of Labor Statistics*. <www.bls.gov/iag/tgs/iag72.htm>
2 Andrea Romano (2018) "The World's Oldest Hotel Has Been in the Same Family for 52 Generations (Video)," 10 August, *Travel + Leisure*. <www.traveland leisure.com/hotels-resorts/japanese-hotel-oldest-in-the-world>
3 Guinness World Records, "Oldest Hotel," *Guinness World Records*.
4 Russell and Dawson, "Evolution of Hospitality Industry," *Russell and Dawson*. <www.rdaep.com/blogs/evolution-hospitality-industry/>
5 Samuel Wich, "The Origins of the Hospitality Industry and What Lies Ahead," *EHL Insights*. <https://hospitalityinsights.ehl.edu/origins-hospitality-industry>
6 Russel and Dawson.
7 U.S. Bureau of Labor Statistics (2019) "Occupational Employment Statistics (OES) Survey," May 2019 OES Estimates, *U.S. Department of Labor, Bureau of Labor Statistics*.
8 Brandon Ambrosino (2014) "Why the Disappearance of Hotel Room Keys Marks the End of Hospitality," 18 February, *Quartz*. <https://qz.com/177505/why-the-disappearance-of-hotel-room-keys-marks-the-end-of-hospitality/>

9 Tony Beck (2007) "Barron's Lock," *The Lock Collectors Association.* <www.lock collectors.eu/members/lockdatabase/bar1/_index.htm>

10 Jane Austen Centre, "Joseph Bramah: Inventor Extraordinaire," *JaneAusten. co.uk.*

11 Jeffrey Kastner (2006) "National Insecurity: A. C. Hobbs and the Great Lock Controversy of 1851," Summer 2006, *Cabinet.*

12 Linus Yale, Jr. (1861) "Lock," Specification of Letters Patent No. 31,278, 29 January 1861, *U.S. Patent Office.*

13 Tor Sornes (1978) "Lock Arrangement Employing Mechanically Acting Code Card and Key Card," Filed 28 March 1978, Application No. 891,390. Patent No. 4,149,394, 17 April 1979, *U.S. Patent and Trademark Office.*

14 Walter Fromm (1974) "Magnetic Door Lock System," Filed 15 May 1974, Application No. 470,188. Patent No. 3,919,869, 18 November 1975, *U.S. Patent and Trademark Office.*

15 MessyNessy (2017) "Oh to Have Eaten at the Automat, Just Once," 4 August, *Cabinet of Chic Curiosities.* <www.messynessychic.com/2017/08/04/ oh-to-have-eaten-at-the-automat-just-once/>

16 Bob Strauss (2021) "The Rise and Fall of the Automat: Whatever Happened to Horn and Hardart?" 31 January 2021, *ThoughtCo.* <www.thoughtco.com/ the-rise-and-fall-of-the-automat-4152992>

17 Kenrick Davis (2020) "Welcome to China's Latest 'Robot Restaurant'," 1 July, *World Economic Forum.* <www.weforum.org/agenda/2020/07/ china-robots-ai-restaurant-hospitality>

18 Katie Sabatini (2019) "Automation Innovation: Cobots and Other Technologies for Your Kitchen," July–August, *Nutrition and Foodservice Edge.* <www.anfp online.org/docs/default-source/legacy-docs/docs/ce-articles/fpc072019.pdf>

19 Anna Wolfe (2019) "3 Reasons Automation Is Redefining Restaurants," 18 October, *Hospitality Technology.* <https://hospitalitytech. com/3-reasons-automation-redefining-restaurants>

20 Sabatini.

Chapter 8

Automation in Health Care

8.1 Chapter Summary

Chapter 8 describes the health care industry sector and the demand for human workers in health care. An historical overview of technological systems in the past is provided. This background of past systems transitions to a review of future technological systems. Based on what has been developed, I predict which future systems would be available in the near and distant future. The chapter concludes with occupations that would be affected and unaffected by business automation brought on by the technological systems designed for the health care sector.

8.2 Description of the Industry

The health care industry sector inclusive of social assistance covers organizations that provide medical care services and/or social assistance services to people. According to the North American Industry Classification System, organizations in this sector are "arranged on a continuum starting with those providing medical care exclusively, continuing with those providing health care and social assistance, and finally finishing with those providing only social assistance."[1] Organizations may operate either as a non-profit organization or as a for-profit corporation. Since this sector does not manufacture products, organizations would have to acquire medical-related machines, devices, equipment, drugs, and supplies from the manufacturing sector.

DOI: 10.4324/9781003189329-9

Organizations in this sector are commonly known as hospitals and primary care clinics. Other names may be nursing homes, hospices, and adult day-care centers. Non-profit organizations may offer a range of social assistance services such as substance-abuse treatment, mental illness counseling, and physical therapy rehabilitation.

Organizations in this sector must be registered with state and local authorities, as there is a risk of an accident that causes injury or death to patients. These organizations would have a governance structure and a management team to plan and oversee operations. Organizations will have state and federal regulations to comply with. Human workers must be adequately trained in their specialized field and in some instances must be licensed or certified by a certification authority.

8.3 Demand for Human Workers

In 2019, the health care sector employed an estimated 21.03 million people across the United States, filling 477 occupations that included a wide range of medical practitioners and support staff necessary to operate health care facilities.[2] This sector had the highest number of people employed (less than 25 percent) of all eight industry sectors studied in this book. Among the top 25 occupations, personal care aides made up the largest occupation at more than 3 million people. The second and third largest occupations had 2.60 million registered nurses and 1.31 million nursing assistants, respectively. Other in-demand occupations included physicians and ophthalmologists, licensed vocational nurses, medical assistants, dental assistants, health services managers, medical secretaries, information clerks, preschool teachers, and childcare workers. Ranked in order of estimated total health care employment, the top 25 occupations were:

1. Home Health and Personal Care Aides (SOC Code: 31–1120)
2. Registered Nurses (SOC Code: 29–1141)
3. Nursing Assistants (SOC Code: 31–1131)
4. Medical Assistants (SOC Code: 31–9092)
5. Licensed Practical and Licensed Vocational Nurses (SOC Code: 29–2061)
6. Medical Secretaries and Administrative Assistants (SOC Code: 43–6013)
7. Receptionists and Information Clerks (SOC Code: 43–4171)

8. Office Clerks, General (SOC Code: 43–9061)

9. Dental Assistants (SOC Code: 31–9091)

10. Childcare Workers (SOC Code: 39–9011)

11. Physicians, All Other; and Ophthalmologists, Except Pediatric (SOC Code: 29–1228)

12. Preschool Teachers, Except Special Education (SOC Code: 25–2011)

13. Medical and Health Services Managers (SOC Code: 11–9111)

14. Clinical Laboratory Technologists and Technicians (SOC Code: 29–2010)

15. Social and Human Service Assistants (SOC Code: 21–1093)

16. Medical Dosimetrists, Medical Records Specialists, and Health Technologists and Technicians, All Other (SOC Code: 29–2098)

17. Maids and Housekeeping Cleaners (SOC Code: 37–2012)

18. First-Line Supervisors of Office and Administrative Support Workers (SOC Code: 43–1011)

19. Substance Abuse, Behavioral Disorder, and Mental Health Counselors (SOC Code: 21–1018)

20. Secretaries and Administrative Assistants, Except Legal, Medical, and Executive (SOC Code: 43–6014)

21. Physical Therapists (SOC Code: 29–1123)

22. Dental Hygienists (SOC Code: 29–1292)

23. Billing and Posting Clerks (SOC Code: 43–3021)

24. Radiologic Technologists and Technicians (SOC Code: 29–2034)

25. Nurse Practitioners (SOC Code: 29–1171)

Of the 477 occupations, 237 occupations were common among six or more industry sectors, making up more than 11 million of total health care employment – more than half of total health care employment. These common occupations are important to note. In the event of a mass layoff, people hired in the 237 occupations could take their knowledge and skills and apply them in another industry sector. For example, receptionists and information clerks, if they found themselves unemployed, could move to the administrative and support sector, the educational services sector, or another industry where they can apply their same skills. Common occupations included personal care aides, registered nurses, emergency medical technicians and paramedics, health services managers, administrative occupations (secretaries and various clerks), cafeteria cooks, food servers, housekeeping cleaners, childcare workers, and first-line supervisors.

8.4 Technological Systems in the Past

A telephone system, invented in 1876 by Alexander Graham Bell, enabled human speech and sound in general to be reproduced across a wire from one person to another, when both persons were located at a far distance where they could not exchange their words in direct face-to-face contact. In other words, two people can through the use of the telephone have a conversation with each other even when they are in different locations. Shortly after the telephone was invented, medical practitioners started using this system and immediately saw how useful it was. "[They] used the technology, which enabled the clear transmission and reproduction of complex sounds for the first time, to improve existing instruments, or to devise entirely new examination methods."[3] The telephone was compared to the stethoscope, which was invented 60 years earlier. An 1879 case published in the *Lancet* described a doctor who was called during the night and asked for the child to be held up to the mouthpiece so that he could hear the child's cough.[4] Since that reported case, "using the telephone to assess [a] patient's medical condition has become a major part of medical practice."[5]

The telephone system facilitated the process of diagnosing an illness, adding another tool that a physician can use. Being able to call a physician from a distance and at any time helped to release some level of anxiety when in the moment the patient needed medical attention the most. During the late 19th century, it would have been difficult or inconvenient to travel to the doctor's office upon the immediate onset of a potentially life-threatening illness. The use of the telephone showed how time can be saved by talking to a doctor over the phone as opposed to visiting a doctor's office.

Over the next several decades, the numbering system used to call a person evolved to be able to issue a unique phone number to an increasingly large number of telephone subscribers. The result led to the current ten-digit phone number. The idea to create a single number that could be simpler for the purpose of calling emergency services had emerged in the mid-1950s. After two studies were released in 1966 and 1967, the digits 9–1–1 were set in 1968 for use as a universal emergency phone number. A system that included dispatchers to handle incoming 911 calls would follow. In the past, individuals had to dial a complicated or unfamiliar long phone number to reach an emergency service or dial 0 for the telephone operator. The simpler three-digit number alleviated the concerns surrounding the use of a long number format.

Communication between the doctor and patient played an important role in understanding and treating illness. From the 16th to the 19th centuries in western Europe, physicians took the time to listen to their patients, writing notes about patients' feelings in notebooks and diaries.[6] Such an activity would have created a strong relationship between the doctor and patient as the two would have developed trust to discuss private and sensitive matters.

When hospitals emerged in the 19th century, medical practitioners started to see a need to formalize patient records so that disease and treatment can be better understood in a systematic way. Thus, the way of documenting patient records from informal notes to formal record-keeping would start to change. The American College of Surgeons established the American Association of Record Librarians of North America in 1928 to standardize clinical records in hospitals and medical institutions. The Association changed its name a few times over the years to become the American Health Information Management Association (AHIMA) in 1991.

Various organizations working independently attempted to design systems and methods to structure health records in a computer-based information system from the late 1960s to the 1970s. Projects would have used either a mainframe computer or a minicomputer. Some projects succeeded while others failed. For those that failed, issues were related to funding, technical limitations, and slow data processing.[7] Known projects included the Eclipsys system by the Lockheed Corporation; the Computer Stored Ambulatory Record at the Massachusetts General Hospital; the Regenstrief Medical Record System by Regenstrief Institute; the Decentralized Hospital Computer Program by the Veterans Administration; and the Health Evaluation through Logical Processing system by a collaborative group made up of the University of Utah, 3M, and the Latter Day Saints Hospital.[8]

The affordability and availability of the personal computer in the 1980s accelerated adoption of recording health records in the computer. Before the advent of the personal computer, implementing a mainframe computer and all the requisite equipment amounted to a high cost that many health care providers could not afford. Software developers found particular pathways (i.e., specific use cases) to introduce electronic health record-keeping. A notable success was in a computer software program that improved the efficiency in registering patients at check-in.[9]

The evolution of electronic health records resulted in interoperability issues – a significant challenge. Because various organizations implemented information systems that met specific and localized business needs, one provider's system could not communicate with another provider's system.

A number of factors would lead to this problem. A health care provider designed a system for use in its facility with no plans to have external organizations have access to the system. Specialized functions in one system were not applicable or relevant to another organization's needs. Software developers built a software program in a particular way that was not compatible with another software program developed by a different software team. The particular computer hardware used by one organization was not compatible with another organization's computer hardware. Network infrastructure was unavailable between organizations.

Issues related to data privacy and patient confidentiality may have posed barriers to sharing patient records between health care providers.

Two international standards were established to ensure that health-related data can be read and interpreted by diverse organizations and systems. The World Health Organization (WHO) oversees development and adoption of the International Statistical Classification of Diseases and Related Health Problems (ICD) to provide systematic recording of mortality, morbidity, diseases, and other health-related data. This standard ensures interoperability and reusability of health data. As of 1 January 2022, the 11th revision (ICD-11) replaces the 10th revision (ICD-10). Health Level Seven International (HL7), a non-profit organization, established a framework and standards for the language, structure, and data types of health-related data to ensure that electronic health records can be integrated in different health information systems.

8.5 Technological Systems in the Future

Various machines and devices have been developed to assist an elderly person to move easily and to access the facilities. Metal handles with soft grips can be attached to a toilet. This simple device allows a person to have something to hold onto while he lowers himself down to and raises himself up from the toilet seat. Handles can also be attached to a conventional bed for a person to be able to raise himself out of bed. A walker is another simple device that aides a person to stand upright and to keep him stable while he walks forward. An electric lift is a machine that aides a person to sit down on and stand up from a chair or couch with minimal pain or discomfort. The lift machine is designed to move up or down a certain number of degrees at an angle. A wheelchair incline lift is a machine designed to convey a person up a flight of stairs. A conveyor system is attached to the wall along the stairs where a platform can slowly move from the bottom to the top. Without any of these assistive technologies, an elderly person has to rely on another person (e.g., a family member or a caregiver) for needed support.

Eating with conventional utensils can be difficult for an elderly person or a person with a disability. A mechanical machine has been developed to rotate and tilt an arm. With a spoon connected to the arm, the machine can pick up food from a plate and raise it up to the level of a person's mouth. Another device aides a person to stabilize her grip so that she has improved movement control with an eating utensil. Without these devices, a person has to rely on another person for assistance in eating a meal.

Measuring a person's vital signs and health can involve a number of instruments such as a thermometer, a pulse monitor, a stethoscope, and a blood pressure machine. Checkme Doctor, developed by Wellue Health, is a portable electronic device equipped with a computer processor, a touch-screen display, sensors, and attachments for electrodes and SpO2 finger sensor to measure a person's temperature, pulse rate, heart rate, and oxygen saturation. A computer software program was developed to retrieve data from the device and display the results of health monitoring.

Emerging in the medical field is the development of nanomedicines and microrobots. These are very tiny machines built from molecules. Nanomedicine is a specific form of intervention designed to cure disease or repair damaged tissue.[10] A microrobot is developed biologically, chemically, or physically to create a motile system.[11]

Performing surgery is becoming minimally invasive, where instead of making a large incision, a small incision is made. Robotic-assisted surgery is a minimally-invasive approach that allows a surgeon to have precise control of surgical instruments whereby the risk to damaging neighboring organs and nerves is reduced. The Da Vinci surgical system is a machine designed with robotic arms that can handle and manipulate tiny instruments. A surgeon sits at a computer console, looking through a viewer that magnifies the interior of the patient's body.

Machines have been developed to facilitate work in pharmacies, hospitals, and laboratories. Automated drug-dispensing machines have been designed to manage drug inventories and to fill a bottle with a certain amount of pills. An autonomous mobile robot, similarly described in previous chapters, has been developed to pick up and deliver various kinds of loads including specimens in hospitals and laboratories. A pre-analytical workstation has been developed to automate several steps in handling lab specimens.

A mobile computer tablet designed to run the same software programs used in a personal computer allows a doctor to record patient information electronically. He can carry it with him as he assists one patient to the next patient, recording and organizing new information in the computer tablet. Since information is in an electronic format, the doctor could transmit the data wirelessly to a computer-based health information system. The mobile computer tablet includes a touch-screen display, a wireless network connection, a camera, a microphone, and a speaker.

A specialized computer software program designed for video-conferencing can be installed in a mobile computer tablet. And if a patient has a computer with a video-conferencing software program, she would be able to connect with her doctor and discuss her situation. The doctor and the patient can be in different locations but can see and talk to each other via the video-conferencing software. The doctor can ask questions and the patient can respond. If the patient has a Checkme device or some other health monitoring device, the doctor could instruct her on using the device to report her vital statistics. The combination of a health monitoring device, computers, and video-conferencing software can create an effective telemedicine session.

8.6 Forecasting of Technological Systems

All of the technological systems except for three systems are available now. Automated drug-dispensing machines would be available within the next 7 years. Autonomous mobile robots specially designed for health care would be available in about 8 to 15 years. Microrobots are still in the experiment stage and may be available in 25 years.

8.7 Changes in Jobs, Roles, and Occupations

Occupations that involve treating, healing, and assisting patients will likely not be eliminated. These workers (doctors, nurses, therapists, various health-related assistants, and personal care aides) making up 11 out of the 25 occupations listed above would see their work improved from future technological systems. As they deal with patients directly, they would be able to focus on working with patients on a more personal level (i.e., talking with patients to provide emotional support that helps them get through pain and suffering). The jobs of doctors, nurses, and therapists would not change but would be made more effective through the use of the new technological systems.

Health services managers, technologists, and technicians would be needed to oversee and manage the implemented technologies. The technicians would be required to operate the new machines. These workers will need to know how the technological systems operate. The jobs of services managers, technologists, and technicians would not change.

The job of medical records specialists would change to focus on data analysis and report generation. They would still be responsible for recording and managing health-related data, but the data-entry work would be made easier with the use of a health information system. The extra time that would be saved in less data entry could be spent to check for data accuracy and to analyze patient records more deeply.

Those occupations related to administering the medical office could be eliminated. The occupations would be receptionists and administrative assistants. Other occupations could be office clerks, information clerks, and billing and posting clerks.

Based on an analysis of a sample of 2019 employment data from the Bureau of Labor Statistics, a small proportion of human workers (6.2 percent) in the health care sector would be displaced by business automation brought on by future technological systems. By a wide margin, more than half of all human workers (53.8 percent) in the health care sector would be unaffected by the new systems. The following 17 occupations would be unaffected or even enhanced by future technological systems:

1. Home Health and Personal Care Aides (SOC Code: 31–1120)
2. Registered Nurses (SOC Code: 29–1141)
3. Nursing Assistants (SOC Code: 31–1131)
4. Medical Assistants (SOC Code: 31–9092)
5. Licensed Practical and Licensed Vocational Nurses (SOC Code: 29–2061)
6. Dental Assistants (SOC Code: 31–9091)
7. Physicians, All Other; and Ophthalmologists, Except Pediatric (SOC Code: 29–1228)
8. Medical and Health Services Managers (SOC Code: 11–9111)
9. Clinical Laboratory Technologists and Technicians (SOC Code: 29–2010)
10. Social and Human Service Assistants (SOC Code: 21–1093)
11. Medical Dosimetrists, Medical Records Specialists, and Health Technologists and Technicians, All Other (SOC Code: 29–2098)

12. Maids and Housekeeping Cleaners (SOC Code: 37–2012)
13. Substance Abuse, Behavioral Disorder, and Mental Health Counselors (SOC Code: 21–1018)
14. Physical Therapists (SOC Code: 29–1123)
15. Dental Hygienists (SOC Code: 29–1292)
16. Radiologic Technologists and Technicians (SOC Code: 29–2034)
17. Nurse Practitioners (SOC Code: 29–1171)

On the other hand, the following four occupations would be affected by future technological systems:

1. Receptionists and Information Clerks (SOC Code: 43–4171)
2. Office Clerks, General (SOC Code: 43–9061)
3. Secretaries and Administrative Assistants, Except Legal, Medical, and Executive (SOC Code: 43–6014)
4. Billing and Posting Clerks (SOC Code: 43–3021)

Notes

1 U.S. Bureau of Labor Statistics (2021) "Industries at a Glance: Health Care and Social Assistance: NAICS 62," 8 January, *U.S. Department of Labor, Bureau of Labor Statistics.* <www.bls.gov/iag/tgs/iag62.htm>
2 U.S. Bureau of Labor Statistics (2019) "Occupational Employment Statistics (OES) Survey," May 2019 OES Estimates, *U.S. Department of Labor, Bureau of Labor Statistics.*
3 Vanessa Rampton, Maria Böhmer, and Anita Winkler (2021) "Medical Technologies Past and Present: How History Helps to Understand the Digital Era," 7 July, *Journal of Medical Humanities.* <https://doi.org/10.1007/s10912-021-09699-x>
4 Rampton.
5 James S. Studdiford et al. (1996) "The Telephone in Primary Care," March, *Primary Care: Clinics in Office Practice*, 23, no. 1.
6 Rampton.
7 Linda Q. Thede and Jeanne P. Sewell (2012) "Computer Development and Health Care Information Systems 1950 to Present," 8 December. Adapted online at http://dlthede.net/informatics/chap01introni/healthcare_computers.html from Jeanne P. Sewell and Linda Q. Thede, *Informatics and Nursing: Opportunities and Challenges.*
8 Micky Tripathi (2012) "EHR Evolution: Policy and Legislation Forces Changing the EHR," October, *Journal of AHIMA*, 83, no. 10.

9 Ashley Brooks (2015) "Health Information Management History: Past, Present and Future," 23 March, *Rasmussen University.* <www.rasmussen.edu/degrees/health-sciences/blog/health-information-management-history/>

10 Thomas J. Webster (2006) "Nanomedicine: What's in a Definition?" June, *International Journal of Nanomedicine*, 1, no. 2.

11 Christine K. Schmidt et al. (2020) "Engineering Microrobots for Targeted Cancer Therapies from a Medical Perspective," 5 November, *Nature Communications*, 11.

Chapter 9

Automation in Administrative and Support

9.1 Chapter Summary

Chapter 9 describes the administrative and support industry sector and the demand for human workers in this sector. An historical overview of technological systems in the past is provided. This background of past systems transitions to a review of future technological systems. Since all of the future systems are available now, this chapter does not include a forecast section like the other chapters. The future of office-related administration is essentially here. The chapter concludes with occupations that would be affected and unaffected by business automation brought on by the technological systems designed for the administrative and support sector.

9.2 Description of the Industry

The administrative and support industry sector covers organizations that provide office-related administration, support services, and waste disposal services. The formal name of this sector as defined by the North American Industry Classification System is "Administrative and Support and Waste Management and Remediation Services."[1] Organizations in this industry sector ensure the proper day-to-day operations of standard business functions such as finance, human resources, and information technology, which serve as the backbone of any organization.

DOI: 10.4324/9781003189329-10

A department or a division is typically found within an existing corporation, non-profit organization, or other type of organization to carry out office-related administration and support services. Common names are Administration Department, Administration and Finance, Finance Department, Human Resources Department, and Information Technology Department.

It would be rare to have an entity that operates solely to provide administration without offering some unique product or service. In such a case, the administrative and support business may be providing its service on contract to other organizations. An example of a stand-alone administrative and support entity is an independent accounting firm. Another example could be a management consulting firm.

9.3 Demand for Human Workers

In 2019, the administrative and support sector employed an estimated 9.37 million people across the United States, filling 624 occupations.[2] Among the top 25 occupations, janitors and cleaners made up the largest occupation at 965,210 people. The second and third largest occupations had 714,630 security guards and 689,880 laborers and stock movers, respectively. Other in-demand occupations included operations managers, office clerks, administrative assistants, human resources specialists, customer service representatives, sales representatives, tractor-trailer truck drivers, assemblers and fabricators, packers and packagers, housekeeping cleaners, and groundskeeping workers. Ranked in order of estimated total sector employment from highest to lowest, the top 25 occupations were:

1. Janitors and Cleaners, Except Maids and Housekeeping Cleaners (SOC Code: 37–2011)
2. Security Guards (SOC Code: 33–9032)
3. Laborers and Freight, Stock, and Material Movers, Hand (SOC Code: 53–7062)
4. Landscaping and Groundskeeping Workers (SOC Code: 37–3011)
5. Customer Service Representatives (SOC Code: 43–4051)
6. Office Clerks, General (SOC Code: 43–9061)
7. Miscellaneous Assemblers and Fabricators (SOC Code: 51–2090)
8. General and Operations Managers (SOC Code: 11–1021)
9. Sales Representatives of Services, Except Advertising, Insurance, Financial Services, and Travel (SOC Code: 41–3091)

10. Packers and Packagers, Hand (SOC Code: 53–7064)
11. Secretaries and Administrative Assistants, Except Legal, Medical, and Executive (SOC Code: 43–6014)
12. Maids and Housekeeping Cleaners (SOC Code: 37–2012)
13. Human Resources Specialists (SOC Code: 13–1071)
14. Heavy and Tractor-Trailer Truck Drivers (SOC Code: 53–3032)
15. Bookkeeping, Accounting, and Auditing Clerks (SOC Code: 43–3031)
16. First-Line Supervisors of Office and Administrative Support Workers (SOC Code: 43–1011)
17. Bill and Account Collectors (SOC Code: 43–3011)
18. Production Workers, All Other (SOC Code: 51–9199)
19. Stockers and Order Fillers (SOC Code: 53–7065)
20. Telemarketers (SOC Code: 41–9041)
21. Helpers – Production Workers (SOC Code: 51–9198)
22. Refuse and Recyclable Material Collectors (SOC Code: 53–7081)
23. Industrial Truck and Tractor Operators (SOC Code: 53–7051)
24. Pest Control Workers (SOC Code: 37–2021)
25. Project Management Specialists and Business Operations Specialists, All Other (SOC Code: 13–1198)

Of the 624 occupations, 247 occupations were common among six or more industry sectors, making up more than 8.27 million people (88 percent of total sector employment). These common occupations are important to note. In the event of a mass layoff, people hired in the 247 occupations could take their knowledge and skills and apply them in another industry sector. For example, human resources specialists, if they found themselves unemployed, could move to the health care sector, the manufacturing sector, or another industry where they can apply their same skills. The top 25 occupations were also the top common occupations. Other common occupations included software developers, computer user support specialists, accountants, inspectors and testers, and maintenance and repair workers.

9.4 Technological Systems in the Past

A significant part of this sector's business is the writing, editing, organization, and management of documents. To carry out the tasks involved in this work, a variety of systems, machines, and tools had been developed over the years.

Writing instruments were implemented to put words down on paper. The graphite pencil traces its roots to 16th-century England where a large deposit of graphite was found. Being brittle, a stick of graphite was wrapped in string or sheepskin to be handled. A stick of graphite later was encased in wood. The term "lead pencil" is a misnomer. A pencil was not made of lead. Old bread was used as an eraser until Joseph Priestley observed in 1770 a substance better suited to remove pencil marks.

The ballpoint pen, first invented by John J. Loud in 1888 and then by László Bíró in 1938, went into production during World War II in Argentina. It would make its way to the United States in 1945. Replacing the fountain pen, the ballpoint pen used a rolling ball at the end and the force of a person's hand to drive viscous ink out of the reservoir and onto the writing material. Before the ballpoint and fountain pens, liquid ink was kept separate in an inkwell. Various dipping tools made from a reed or a bird's feather or attached with a metal nib were used to hold a small amount of ink at the tip, which then can be used to write words on paper. Every so often, the tool would be dipped in the inkwell to take another small amount of ink. Both the fountain pen and ballpoint pen eliminated the inkwell, making it possible to hold a supply of ink within a single instrument.

Marketing and a change in a cultural value would make the typewriter acceptable to most people. "Americans in the 1870s and 1880s were deeply uncomfortable with the strange notion of 'mechanical writing.'"[3] Writing by hand was the convention. And good penmanship was a source of pride that exhibited elegance and grace in more ways beyond the written message. The typewriter would find an audience with the emerging theory called scientific management.[4]

Various models of the typewriter were made, but they all followed the functional design created by Christopher Latham Sholes in 1868. The typewriter was a mechanical machine that comprised an inked ribbon, a cylinder, a carriage, an escapement to control letter spacing, and keys and typebars corresponding to the letters of the alphabet. The typebars were so arranged to strike a center point by using a lever action. The typewriter made it possible to type a lengthy essay on several sheets of paper faster than writing it by hand. It increased the productivity of an office clerk.

A word processor machine improved the functionality of a typewriter by allowing typed text to be edited. In a typewriter, every character was made permanent once it struck the paper. The word processor machine added an electronic circuit, a display screen, and memory capacity. Some models included a device to store typed text on magnetic tape or a floppy disk.

The new functions allowed a typist to move back a number of characters, change the text, and then commit the entered text to paper. The word processor improved on the level of quality in producing a letter by being able to make corrections at the instant that words were typed. The word processor machine came out in the 1960s.

A computer software program was developed in the 1980s to write and edit documents in a computer. This specialized software program allowed a person to do the functions designed in the typewriter and word processor machines and more functions such as using a different typeface, setting the font size, stylizing text with certain effects, and creating a bullet list or numbered list. And then the software allowed the completed document to be saved as an electronic file, which would be sent to a printer for printing on paper. All of the functions were programmed in the software.

The word processing software program saved time and paper by being able to write and edit a full and complete draft a number of times before actually printing a single character on paper. With a typewriter and a word processor machine, numerous sheets of paper would have been used, revision after revision. With the software, printing can wait until a person has thoroughly edited the work and corrected all mistakes to produce a complete and perfect draft.

The process of making copies of an original document evolved over the decades. A sheet of carbon paper was inserted between two sheets of typing paper; and then when used in a typewriter, the bottom typing paper received a duplicate image transferred from the carbon paper. Developed in the late 1870s, a mimeograph machine used a stencil through which ink was pressed to make duplicate prints. Developed in the 1900s, a photostat machine used a camera to capture an original document on sensitized photographic paper to create a negative image, and then the camera was used again on the negative image to create a duplicate print on sensitized photographic paper. A Xerox photocopy machine, invented by Chester Carlson in 1938, applied a six-step electrophotographic process to duplicate an image of an original document by using positive and negative electrical charges. Without these machines to make hundreds or thousands of copies, an office clerk would have to retype the original document over and over again to produce all the required copies. The copying machines made such additional work unnecessary.

In the late 1980s and 1990s, a particular management information system called an enterprise resource planning (ERP) system emerged to support organizations in the areas of finance and accounting, human resources, and inventory. This information system can be traced back to the 1960s where it first was implemented in the manufacturing sector. The ERP system enabled an organization to manage all of its records across multiple business functions in a single database, giving senior management the ability to view the progress of operations in an efficient manner. Without such a system, each department would be managing its own set of records pertinent to its functional area. Senior management then would have to go to each department director to receive progress reports. The ERP system streamlined the process so that all departments can enter and report information in one system. The ERP system comprised a relational database management system, a number of computer servers to store and process data for hundreds or thousands of employees, and a number of computer software components programmed to enter, process, and report a variety of business functions. The ERP system operated in a computer network where employees had access to it from their computers.

9.5 Technological Systems in the Future

Removing germs in numerous rooms and offices can take some time with human workers. Xenex, a start-up company, has made the process of killing pathogens more efficient. Its disinfection machine has been engineered to zap germs by using pulses of ultraviolet (UV) light from a xenon lamp. With motion sensors, the machine will stop disinfecting the room when it detects motion.

An autonomous mobile robot has been developed that could perform like an administrative assistant. Standing at 3.2 feet tall, Temi, developed by a start-up company under the same name, is similar to the other autonomous mobile robots that were described in previous chapters. It can freely move and learn where it has traveled. Temi has a tablet-sized touch-screen display for a person to interact with the software program. A small tray is available to hold light loads. This particular mobile robot comes with a software development kit for software developers to create additional functionalities. A law firm has used Temi to deliver documents to staff and to talk with employees and office visitors via the robot's video-conferencing software. A lawyer at the firm was described as having being able to save 45 minutes from his daily routine working in the office.[5]

The quality and output of speech recognition software programs were poor in the 1990s. But with faster computer processors and better microphones, speech recognition has greatly improved. Human resource software programs have recently been developed to use speech recognition.[6] Instead of accessing HR policies, benefits, time sheets, and other HR functions with a keyboard and mouse, an employee can speak into the computer, and the speech-enabled HR software can return the function as requested. The added functionality would make it easier to navigate and sort through HR records.

Another application for speech recognition software would be to convert the speaker's words into written type. In the past, a person used an audio tape recorder and then transcribed the recording in longhand or on a type-writer or computer. The step of transcribing by hand can be eliminated by a dictation software program. The dictation software program uses speech recognition to record the speaker's words and converts the digital audio into text characters. The dictation software works with a word processing soft-ware program to have the converted text written in the document. A person will see the text appear automatically. And then the person can read what was written and make any edits. The amount of time to create the document has been reduced by not needing to start with a blank document to type the recording manually.

A document automation software program streamlines work flow pro-cesses to draft and assemble various different documents. An organization would have documents that use different structure, formatting, and styling. A certain type of document may require a particular format. Document automation allows an employee to access the right document type by using templates and questionnaires. All of an organization's document types are added in the software to create a template of each added document type. Each template would have markups to indicate where all the parts (e.g., title, headings, and sections) are to be placed on the document. Questionnaires are created to enable the software to select the right template. When an employee answers the questions in a questionnaire, the software can select the template based on the employee's answers.

A document management system enables an organization to store all of its documents in one system. A wide range of electronic files (e.g., a word processing document, a spreadsheet, a PDF document, a scanned image, and an audio recording) can be stored. A version control functionality may be available where employees who store the same document can be distin-guished with a unique version number. Employees can access the system to search and retrieve existing documents and add new documents. The docu-ment management system comprises a computer server, a database system, and a software program, all of which may operate in a remote location accessible via the Internet.

9.6 Occupations Affected and Unaffected

Based on an analysis of a sample of 2019 employment data from the Bureau of Labor Statistics, more than a third of human workers (36 percent) in the administrative and support sector would be displaced by business automation brought on by future technological systems. Less than one-fifth of human workers (19.5 percent) in the administrative and support sector would be unaffected by the new systems. The following nine occupations would be unaffected by future technological systems:

1. Landscaping and Groundskeeping Workers (SOC Code: 37–3011)
2. Customer Service Representatives (SOC Code: 43–4051)
3. Sales Representatives of Services, Except Advertising, Insurance, Financial Services, and Travel (SOC Code: 41–3091)
4. Human Resources Specialists (SOC Code: 13–1071)
5. Bookkeeping, Accounting, and Auditing Clerks (SOC Code: 43–3031)
6. First-Line Supervisors of Office and Administrative Support Workers (SOC Code: 43–1011)
7. Refuse and Recyclable Material Collectors (SOC Code: 53–7081)
8. Pest Control Workers (SOC Code: 37–2021)
9. Project Management Specialists and Business Operations Specialists, All Other (SOC Code: 13–1198)

On the other hand, the following 11 occupations would be affected by future technological systems:

1. Janitors and Cleaners, Except Maids and Housekeeping Cleaners (SOC Code: 37–2011)
2. Security Guards (SOC Code: 33–9032)
3. Laborers and Freight, Stock, and Material Movers, Hand (SOC Code: 53–7062)
4. Office Clerks, General (SOC Code: 43–9061)
5. Packers and Packagers, Hand (SOC Code: 53–7064)
6. Secretaries and Administrative Assistants, Except Legal, Medical, and Executive (SOC Code: 43–6014)
7. Bill and Account Collectors (SOC Code: 43–3011)
8. Production Workers, All Other (SOC Code: 51–9199)
9. Stockers and Order Fillers (SOC Code: 53–7065)
10. Telemarketers (SOC Code: 41–9041)
11. Helpers – Production Workers (SOC Code: 51–9198)

Notes

1 U.S. Bureau of Labor Statistics (2021) "Industries at a Glance: Administrative and Support and Waste Management and Remediation Services: NAICS 56," 8 January, *U.S. Department of Labor, Bureau of Labor Statistics*. <www.bls.gov/iag/tgs/iag56.htm>

2 U.S. Bureau of Labor Statistics (2019) "Occupational Employment Statistics (OES) Survey," May 2019 OES Estimates, *U.S. Department of Labor, Bureau of Labor Statistics*.

3 Smithsonian Education (1998) "Carbons to Computers: Typewriters," *Smithsonian Institution*. <www.smithsonianeducation.org/scitech/carbons/typewriters.html>

4 Smithsonian Education.

5 Nicole Lewis (2020) "Using Robots in the Coronavirus Era," 28 April, *SHRM*. <www.shrm.org/resourcesandtools/hr-topics/technology/pages/using-robots-coronavirus-era.aspx>

6 Dave Zielinski (2019) "HR and Voice Recognition Technology: HR Industry Vendors Have Started Moving Their Voice-activated Applications into Real-world Use," 28 August, *SHRM*. <www.shrm.org/hr-today/news/hr-magazine/fall2019/pages/hr-and-voice-recognition-technology.aspx>

Chapter 10

Automation in Educational Services

10.1 Chapter Summary

Chapter 10 describes the educational services industry sector and the demand for human workers in education. An historical overview of technological systems in the past is provided. This background of past systems transitions to a review of future technological systems. Based on what has been developed, I predict which future systems would be available in the near and distant future. The chapter concludes with occupations that would be affected and unaffected by business automation brought on by the technological systems designed for the educational services sector.

10.2 Description of the Industry

The educational services industry sector covers organizations that provide training to people. Training may include a wide range of subjects. This sector generally does not produce a product but provides a service. According to the North American Industry Classification System, "educational services are usually delivered by teachers or instructors that explain, tell, demonstrate, supervise, and direct learning."[1] Recipients of training span the full age range from children in elementary school to adults in college and vocational school.

Organizations in this sector are commonly known as schools, colleges, and universities. They can also be referred to as vocational schools, trade

DOI: 10.4324/9781003189329-11

schools, and training centers. They may operate as a for-profit corporation or a non-profit organization. Certain schools and colleges may be funded and controlled by a government agency.

There would be certain standards on course curriculum, student testing, and instructor qualifications that organizations must meet. Standards may be mandated by government or directed by a local authority or a non-profit organization. Organizations may be required to establish and maintain accreditation by a government agency or a non-profit organization.

The modes of training can vary. Typically, students attend classes and interact with the instructor and their peers in an in-person environment. Individuals may also complete courses remotely via correspondence, television broadcast, video recording, and most recently via the Internet. Teaching course lessons may entail a combination of modes that includes in-person class attendance and remote learning.

10.3 Demand for Human Workers

In 2019, the educational services sector employed an estimated 13.28 million people across the United States, filling 583 various occupations.[2] This sector employed the third highest number of people, exceeding just ahead of the manufacturing sector. Among the top 25 occupations, elementary school teachers made up the largest occupation at 1.42 million people. The second and third largest occupations had 1.15 million teaching assistants and 1.03 million secondary school teachers, respectively. Other in-demand occupations included postsecondary teachers, middle school teachers, substitute teachers, tutors, career counselors, education administrators, administrative assistants, office clerks, janitors and cleaners, and passenger vehicle drivers. Ranked in order of estimated total educational services employment from highest to lowest, the top 25 occupations were:

1. Elementary School Teachers, Except Special Education (SOC Code: 25–2021)
2. Teaching Assistants, Except Postsecondary (SOC Code: 25–9045)
3. Secondary School Teachers, Except Special and Career/Technical Education (SOC Code: 25–2031)
4. Middle School Teachers, Except Special and Career/Technical Education (SOC Code: 25–2022)

5. Substitute Teachers, Short-Term (SOC Code: 25–3031)
6. Secretaries and Administrative Assistants, Except Legal, Medical, and Executive (SOC Code: 43–6014)
7. Janitors and Cleaners, Except Maids and Housekeeping Cleaners (SOC Code: 37–2011)
8. Office Clerks, General (SOC Code: 43–9061)
9. Education Administrators, Kindergarten through Secondary (SOC Code: 11–9032)
10. Educational, Guidance, and Career Counselors and Advisors (SOC Code: 21–1012)
11. Tutors and Teachers and Instructors, All Other (SOC Code: 25–3097)
12. Passenger Vehicle Drivers, Except Bus Drivers, Transit and Intercity (SOC Code: 53–3058)
13. Postsecondary Teachers, All Other (SOC Code: 25–1199)
14. Health Specialties Teachers, Postsecondary (SOC Code: 25–1071)
15. Special Education Teachers, Kindergarten and Elementary School (SOC Code: 25–2052)
16. Fast Food and Counter Workers (SOC Code: 35–3023)
17. Coaches and Scouts (SOC Code: 27–2022)
18. Self-Enrichment Teachers (SOC Code: 25–3021)
19. Education Administrators, Postsecondary (SOC Code: 11–9033)
20. Instructional Coordinators (SOC Code: 25–9031)
21. Special Education Teachers, Secondary School (SOC Code: 25–2058)
22. Teaching Assistants, Postsecondary (SOC Code: 25–9044)
23. Cooks, Institution and Cafeteria (SOC Code: 35–2012)
24. Childcare Workers (SOC Code: 39–9011)
25. Kindergarten Teachers, Except Special Education (SOC Code: 25–2012)

Of the 583 occupations, 246 occupations were common among six or more industry sectors, making up 4.36 million of total educational services employment. These common occupations are important to note. In the event of a mass layoff, people hired in the 246 occupations could take their knowledge and skills and apply them in another industry sector. For example, secretaries and administrative assistants, if they found themselves unemployed, could move to the health care sector, the administrative and support sector, or another industry where they can apply their same skills. Most common occupations were not teachers but those related to administration and support. Common occupations included instructional coordinators, tutors, childcare workers, secretaries and administrative assistants, office clerks, maintenance and repair workers, janitors and cleaners, passenger vehicle drivers, fast food and counter workers, and cafeteria cooks.

What is striking about this sector is the high number of unique occupations. The educational services sector employed 755,300 people in 44 unique occupations – the highest of all eight industry sectors studied in this book. All other sectors had numbers of unique occupations in the single digit. In terms of number of workers, the transportation and warehousing sector came in second with 580,280 people employed in unique occupations.

The distinguishing characteristic is the wide range of subjects taught by postsecondary teachers. Unique occupations covered specific subjects such as business, education, psychology, engineering, biological science, computer science, and mathematical science.

10.4 Technological Systems in the Past

Many tools had been developed to improve teaching and learning. From the late 16th century to the late 18th century, a hornbook aided in literacy and was used at a time when books were expensive. In the early 19th century, a sandbox was given to each pupil to practice his lessons individually. The sandbox was an inexpensive tool that allowed a pupil to use his finger to write in the sand. Use of a slate replaced the sandbox where a piece of chalk was used to write on the slate. In both cases of using the sandbox and slate, a teacher was able to observe individual performance. By the mid-19th century, a large blackboard allowed a teacher to write and teach lessons to the entire group of pupils. After the turn of the 20th century, paper and graphite pencils became less expensive and gradually replaced slates. In the 20th century, various machines such as a film strip projector, a film projector, an overhead projector, a television, and a video cassette player were introduced in schools and used as part of teaching aides or to enhance the learning experience.

In the early 19th century, Joseph Lancaster designed an efficient method to teach a large group of students. During this time period, one-room schoolhouses were operated where all students from Grade 1 to Grade 8 were in attendance. The "Lancastrian monitorial system of instruction" relied on a group of monitors who were older students to assist the sole teacher. Every morning, the teacher would explain the day's lesson to the monitors. The monitors then worked with a small group of students. Each monitor was assigned ten students. Teaching involved a reward-punishment model where monitors had some degree of authority to promote those who did well and to embarrass those who did poorly. Lancaster authored a book to explain his teaching method and process of teaching reading.

In the 1960s, a teaching machine developed by B. F. Skinner was used in classrooms. His mechanical machine used a paper disc printed with a series of questions and answers. A wide range of paper discs could be developed to teach many subjects. Each paper disc followed a coherent lesson for one particular subject. The machine displayed one question at a time, and the student wrote her answer on paper tape in an area on top of the machine. The student turned a knob to advance the paper disc to show the correct answer. Skinner's teaching machine enabled a student to learn at her own pace, making sure that she can learn the subject. Seeing the correct answer immediately provided a way for the student to know whether she understood the question or not. The student can go through the questions faster or slower, depending on her level of understanding of the subject. The teacher would be able to observe and measure each student's performance and assist those who were struggling with the subject.

With the establishment of the Public Broadcasting Service (PBS) in 1969, content providers have been given an outlet to present television programs that are both entertaining and educational. The widely known program, "Sesame Street," is an example. Educational television created a new genre that combined quality film and video production with quality education. Many shows that were first aired on PBS stations were subsequently used in the classrooms to complement the curriculum. Along with a video cassette copy of the television program, supplemental instruction guides were developed and distributed to serve as teaching aides. A teacher used a television and a video cassette player to show the educational program on video. Afterward, the teacher would have a discussion with students on what they watched. Few studies had been done to evaluate the impact on the use of educational television in the classroom. But what was concluded so far is that when the content of the television program supports the curriculum, the teacher, the viewing context, and learning materials, then learning from television can be effective.[3]

Reviewing and scoring tests is a time-consuming task. A teacher has to go through each and every test taken by her students, identifying and marking incorrect answers. An automated test scoring machine, invented by Michael Sokolski and Thomas J. Poole in 1975, eliminated the need for a teacher to review multiple-choice tests by hand. This machine used light, photosensors, and amplifiers to detect darkened marks on a pre-defined test sheet. A master test sheet showing correctly darkened marks in their designated spaces was fed into the machine to store the correct answers in memory. Subsequent students' test sheets were fed into the machine one by one. The test scoring machine automatically compared a student's test sheet with the master test sheet and printed a mark for any space that did not match. All those printed marks indicated incorrect answers. The machine finally kept a count of correct answers and printed the number on the student's test sheet. An important note about this machine is that it could not score open-ended questions that required a written response. Nevertheless, since its development, this automated test scoring machine has been used widely in schools and colleges across the United States. Readers will know it be its name: Scan-Tron.

10.5 Technological Systems in the Future

Twenty to 40 percent of the time that a teacher spends could be automated, according to McKinsey and Company.[4] Course preparation, course administration, student evaluation, and obtaining feedback are areas that a teacher spends her time. McKinsey concluded that these areas have the potential to be automated.

An automated essay scoring system is designed to evaluate long-form written responses. Various computer-based systems have been developed, using different techniques.[5] Statistical methods are used to compute the mechanics of writing (e.g., grammar, punctuation, and diction). Latent semantic analysis relies on word usage and is used to compute the meaning of words to arrive at the meaning of a passage in an essay. Natural language processing is employed to evaluate an essay by the way certain words, phrases, and clauses are used. An essay scoring system may be trained on a sample of scored essays before it actually evaluates a student essay. Another essay scoring system may have a database of scored essays and other text with which a student essay can be compared against. Employing an automated essay scoring system reduces the amount of time that a teacher has to spend on reviewing student essays.

A customized textbook software program facilitates the process of compiling and preparing textbooks and learning materials in a coherent structure. In the past, an instructor would create a reader composed of a variety of book excerpts, journal articles, and news articles. With the textbook software, the instructor can search a database of books, articles, and other materials and select and organize those items that are relevant to a particular course. The software may have a function to add the instructor's own materials such as classroom exercises, presentation slides, and lecture notes. The software will finally prepare the selected materials in a book format for print or electronic distribution.

An adaptive learning system is designed to adapt a course to a student's progress, ability, and behavior. The conventional way of teaching teaches all students in the same manner without regard to any particular student's learning style. Adaptive learning learns about an individual student and changes the pacing of the course and the sequence of the lessons to be a better fit for the individual student. The next lesson the student sees will be based on how well she did on the previous lesson. The computer software program applies a mathematical model to analyze multiple variables indicating the student's knowledge and behavior. The results of the analysis will then instruct the software to alter the course's design.

An intelligent tutoring system is similar to adaptive learning but has a formal teaching approach. The intelligent tutoring system comprises a knowledge domain model, a pedagogical model, and a learner model.[6] The objective is to ensure that a student has achieved mastery of the course subject through a structured process. The learning objectives for a given course are configured in the system. And formative assessment is continuously applied to check whether the student is learning the subject and to guide where the student needs to go next. The system can advance the student to a lesson of greater difficulty or move the student back to an easier lesson. Several courses covering an educational program or curriculum can be configured in the system. Then the system through formative assessments can direct and track the student's progression through the entire educational program. Since the system considers the student's learning style, the progression of one student can be faster or slower than the progression of another student. The intelligent tutoring system adapts to the student to ensure that she has grasped the concepts of the lesson.

10.6 Forecasting of Technological Systems

The customized textbook software, adaptive learning system, and intelligent tutoring system are available now. The automated essay scoring system would need more development to ensure that scoring is accurate. It may be accurate in identifying grammar mistakes, punctuation, and word usage, but this is just one part of grading an essay. Another part is judging the ideas, facts, commentary, and level of persuasion in the essay. Within the next 7 years, an automated essay scoring system capable of evaluating essays in low-stakes situations (e.g., project essays and short papers) would be available. This early model of an automated essay scoring system would allow the public to review the system's accuracy and provide feedback. Based on public comments, further improvements can be made that results in a system that education administrators can feel confident in. An automated essay scoring system that can be used to evaluate essays for final examination and college admission (high-stakes situations) would be available in about 8 to 15 years.

10.7 Changes in Jobs, Roles, and Occupations

Instructional coordinators and teaching assistants would be impacted by future technological systems. These occupations could be eliminated or significantly reduced in number.

All of the teacher occupations from kindergarten to postsecondary education would not be eliminated. The teacher occupations are so specialized that it will take a long time for technologies to replicate teaching. With technological systems available to do the administrative work, teachers can focus on their primary role, which is to be an educator. They can focus on their job to help students master the subjects at hand.

Education administrators and guidance counselors will be able to see their work improved and overall educational goals achieved. The intelligent tutoring system and adaptive learning system would be able to generate the reports that administrators and counselors need to see student progress both at the individual level and at the aggregated level. Administrators would be able to make better decisions based on the data from those systems. Counselors would be able to make better recommendations that guide students toward meeting their short- and long-term goals.

Based on an analysis of a sample of 2019 employment data from the Bureau of Labor Statistics, a small proportion of human workers (10.7 percent) in the educational services sector would be displaced by business automation brought on by future technological systems. By a wide margin, 43.7 percent of human workers would be unaffected by the new systems. The following 16 occupations would be unaffected by future technological systems:

1. Elementary School Teachers, Except Special Education (SOC Code: 25–2021)
2. Secondary School Teachers, Except Special and Career/Technical Education (SOC Code: 25–2031)

3. Middle School Teachers, Except Special and Career/Technical Education (SOC Code: 25–2022)
4. Substitute Teachers, Short-Term (SOC Code: 25–3031)
5. Education Administrators, Kindergarten through Secondary (SOC Code: 11–9032)
6. Educational, Guidance, and Career Counselors and Advisors (SOC Code: 21–1012)
7. Tutors and Teachers and Instructors, All Other (SOC Code: 25–3097)
8. Postsecondary Teachers, All Other (SOC Code: 25–1199)
9. Health Specialties Teachers, Postsecondary (SOC Code: 25–1071)
10. Special Education Teachers, Kindergarten and Elementary School (SOC Code: 25–2052)
11. Coaches and Scouts (SOC Code: 27–2022)
12. Self-Enrichment Teachers (SOC Code: 25–3021)
13. Education Administrators, Postsecondary (SOC Code: 11–9033)
14. Special Education Teachers, Secondary School (SOC Code: 25–2058)
15. Cooks, Institution and Cafeteria (SOC Code: 35–2012)
16. Kindergarten Teachers, Except Special Education (SOC Code: 25–2012)

On the other hand, the following three occupations would be affected by future technological systems:

1. Teaching Assistants, Except Postsecondary (SOC Code: 25–9045)
2. Instructional Coordinators (SOC Code: 25–9031)
3. Teaching Assistants, Postsecondary (SOC Code: 25–9044)

Notes

1 U.S. Bureau of Labor Statistics (2021) "Industries at a Glance: Educational Services: NAICS 61," 8 January, *U.S. Department of Labor, Bureau of Labor Statistics.* <www.bls.gov/iag/tgs/iag61.htm>
2 U.S. Bureau of Labor Statistics (2019) "Occupational Employment Statistics (OES) Survey," May 2019 OES Estimates, *U.S. Department of Labor, Bureau of Labor Statistics.*
3 Babette Moeller (1996) "Learning from Television: A Research Review," CCT Reports, Issue No. 11, October, *Education Development Center, Center for Children and Technology*; Center for Children and Technology (2004) "Television Goes to School: The Impact of Video on Student Learning in Formal Education," January, *Corporation for Public Broadcasting.* <https://dcmp.org/learn/static-assets/nadh173.pdf>

4 Jake Bryant et al. (2020) "How Artificial Intelligence Will Impact K-12 Teachers," 14 January, *McKinsey and Company.* <www.mckinsey.com/industries/public-and-social-sector/our-insights/how-artificial-intelligence-will-impact-k-12-teachers>

5 Semire Dikli (2006) "An Overview of Automated Scoring of Essays," August, *Journal of Technology, Learning, and Assessment,* 5, no. 1.

6 Kelly Walsh (2019) "Intelligent Tutoring Systems (a Decades-old Application of AI in Education)," 3 December, *EmergingEdTech.com.* <www.emergingedtech.com/2019/12/intelligent-tutoring-systems-application-of-ai-in-education/>

Chapter 11

Widespread Automation Across the Economy

11.1 Chapter Summary

Chapter 11 summarizes the technological systems described in the preceding eight chapters to find similarities that systems share across multiple industries. Notable differences in the technological systems are highlighted. The forecasts of when systems would be implemented are analyzed to create a composite view of eight industry sectors. A timeline of all sectors in one view illustrates those sectors that would automate sooner and those sectors that would automate later. Reasons for why certain industries will be slower than others are provided. Leaders and laggard sectors are identified. The chapter concludes with a summary of how business automation will unfold to spread across all industry sectors.

11.2 Similarities of Future Technological Systems

With the exception of the administrative and support sector and the educational services sector, hardware is a dominant feature in future technological systems. Modernizing past systems require incorporating the computer and electronic parts into the mechanics of a machine. In cases where no previous machines existed, completely new hardware systems need to be developed. Servo motors are used to control the movement of arms with greater precision. Sensors are used to collect information about the surrounding

DOI: 10.4324/9781003189329-12

environment. A computer is used to process data and to control the parts of the system.

Two broad categories of hardware machines are being developed across multiple industry sectors. In one category, a technological system moves freely inside a building or outside in an open field. In the other category, a technological system stays fixed in one location. Collaborative robots in most cases remain stationary with only their arms to move in particular ways. A collaborative robot designed to make manufacturing parts would stay in place. A collaborative robot designed to cook meals would also stay in place.

An autonomous mobile robot, an autonomous vehicle, and a self-propelled vehicle come equipped with wheels and a navigation method to roam around. No longer are these systems constrained by being used in one location. They can move in certain distances away from their home. Movement would be limited by the particular form of navigation used. Some vehicles may be constrained to follow along a pre-defined path. Other vehicles may move in any direction that is controlled remotely by a human operator. More advanced vehicles may be equipped with maps, cameras, and additional sensors to detect where the vehicle has traveled so far and to process where it should go next.

A common theme that the autonomous mobile robots share across multiple industries is the unique functions for which the individual machines are designed to do. Despite having similar components, an autonomous mobile robot is designed for a specific application based on specific needs. For example, an autonomous weeding machine uses a chemical sprayer to kill weeds. An autonomous waiter robot uses a tray to deliver a hot meal. Each autonomous mobile robot handles a particular task. Each robot is configured to do something different. As such, autonomous mobile robots are not interchangeable that can be used for other purposes.

The specialization of mobile robots logically follows the specialization of occupations. Workers have been hired to do particular tasks. When one worker is no longer able to complete the specific tasks, another worker has to be hired or trained to do those specific tasks. The employer goes through a process to find the right worker who can do those specific tasks very well. Technological development builds on this convention to produce highly specialized autonomous mobile robots. Rather than searching for a specialized worker to do specific tasks, an employer looks for a specialized robot.

11.3 Notable Developments in Future Technological Systems

Four technological developments are worth pointing out. Competing approaches to develop autonomous vehicles are playing out in the transportation and construction sectors. One approach focuses on computer software and electronics to control the mechanics of a car or truck. The other approach relies on teleoperation to control the mechanics remotely. The latter approach uses a human who is located in an office miles away from the vehicle. Both approaches eliminate the need to have a person inside the vehicle. They both are achieving the same objective, but they are doing so with a different method.

The second development is the concept of platooning. This new method would replace the current method of attaching multiple trailers to a single cab. Regulations in certain states limit the number of trailers that can be attached. The platooning of multiple trucks would serve a similar purpose of hauling two or more trailers. A number of individual trucks can be linked together with wireless technology and yet not be physically connected. A freight company would be capable of transporting multiple cargo loads safely and efficiently by using the platooning method.

Operating several autonomous vehicles or robots in a swarm is another notable technological development. In the agriculture and construction sectors, wide open space is available. Certain specific tasks require a number of workers of the same occupation to cover the available area. For example, several chemical applicators would be needed to cover tens of acres of land. Several drywall installers would be needed to cover all the floors of a tall building. Several autonomous vehicles or robots would be orchestrated to complete the specialized tasks and cover the entire area with greater efficiency and quality. The identical machines would apply the work in a uniform manner. All of the machines would start at the same time and would be instructed to move to a designated area where each machine carries out the work.

The last notable development is microrobots. It is still too early to state precisely what these molecular machines could do. In theory, the microrobot can be a form of medical intervention that can be less intrusive than surgery. The microrobot could detect and treat a disease inside the human body more effectively than current medical treatments.

11.4 Timeline for Automating Industry Sectors

Figure 11.1 illustrates how long all eight industry sectors would take to implement available technologies for automation. The chart provides a composite view of all the forecasts made in the preceding eight chapters. From now to 25 years, organizations in their respective sector would be able to improve the efficiency of their operations by purchasing and using technological systems. Some systems as forecasted may not be available for technical, legal, or other reasons. The percentage of systems that will be available represent those that are technically mature and stable, which would have minimal disruption to current business operations. The timeline of available technologies is broken down to four time periods: (1) available now, (2) within 7 years, (3) from 8 to 15 years, and (4) from 16 to 25 years. The base reference year from which the timeline starts is 2021. The ending year of the timeline is 2046.

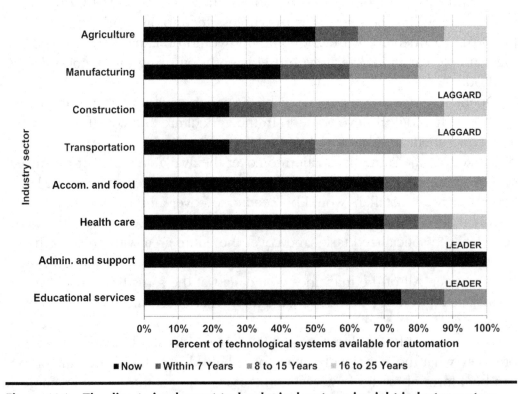

Figure 11.1   Timeline to implement technological systems in eight industry sectors.

Source: Author's analysis of various technological systems described in previous chapters.

The administrative and support sector and the educational services sector would be the first and second leaders, respectively, to automate sooner than later. These two industries rely mostly on computer software, unlike the other sectors. Organizations would not have to make a significant investment on physical hardware. They could use existing computers so long as the computers meet the technical requirements of the software systems.

All of the technological systems designed for the administrative and support sector are available. The software systems designed for the educational services sector are available now. The remaining system to score essays would be implemented in phases within 7–15 years. An automated essay scoring system for low-stakes applications (e.g., project essays) would be ready sooner than an automated essay scoring system for high-stakes applications (e.g., college admission). Technical issues still need to be worked out to ensure that the scoring system can accurately grade written responses. Scoring essays is not as simple as scoring multiple choice selections.

A cultural issue would affect when high-stakes essay scoring systems are deployed. Students and parents will want to make sure that essay-based examinations are scored fairly. Parents would have an influence on whether or not the technology is used in practice.

The accommodation and food services sector would be the third industry to automate. Most of its technological systems are available now. Collaborative robot cooks would take a longer time to include all the possible variety of meals and cooking techniques. Specialized robot cooks to prepare soups, vegetable dishes, desserts, baked goods, and cultural cuisines still need to be developed. The complexity of heating, ventilation, and air-conditioning systems would take a while to create a fully automated heating, ventilation, and air-conditioning (HVAC) system that is smart enough to control all aspects of the mechanical parts.

Despite the availability of the matured technologies, some organizations may be slower than others to adopt a smart HVAC system, robot cooks, and other hardware systems. Purchasing and installing hardware systems will be an investment that some restaurants and hotels may not be able to afford. Business managers will need to plan an amount of time to install and test the new hardware and train employees on how to use the new machines. Large-scale establishments would be able to commit the time and resources. Small, family-owned businesses may not be able to make the same commitment. Small-sized businesses may not be able to afford the hardware systems.

The health care sector would follow shortly behind the accommodation and food services sector. The innovation of microrobots would take the entire timeline in order for microrobots to reach a level for practical use. Microrobots would also need approval from a government agency for regulatory and safety reasons. Such regulatory approval will take time. The automated drug dispensers would be further developed and made available within 7 years. Development of autonomous mobile robots for health-related purposes could take longer to reach maturity in 8–15 years.

The agriculture sector would gradually reach full automation as technological systems are made available across the timeline. Computerized tractors, variable rate implements, and unmanned aerial vehicles would automate farming tasks. Automated harvesting machines capable of picking and sorting a wide variety of crops still need to be developed. Harvesting machines would be made available within 7 years and 8–15 years, depending on the selected crops and on how successful the machines will be at picking and sorting the crops. A different automated harvester will need to be developed for a specific crop. Autonomous vehicles operating in a swarm would take the longest to ensure the software component can communicate with and coordinate all of the individual vehicles.

Adoption of hardware-based systems can take a longer time for many small-scale farmers and ranchers. Purchasing the new technological systems will be a significant investment. Large-scale agricultural producers would be able to afford the new systems. Small-scale farmers may not.

Like the agriculture sector, the manufacturing sector would gradually automate as technological systems are made available. The warehouse of a manufacturer can be fully automated now with the combination of guided vehicles, mobile robots, and automatic palletizers. Development of light industrial trucks and collaborative robots would take a longer time. Legal issues would need to be resolved to use fully automated light industrial trucks on public roads. All the possible robots to do a wide range of specialized manufacturing tasks still need to be developed.

The transportation sector would be the penultimate industry to automate. Technical development still remains for cars and trucks to rely on software and electronics for full autonomous driving. Autonomous trains would be among the first autonomous vehicles to be available for mass transportation. Autonomous shuttles in restricted operating areas would follow closely behind or emerge as the first autonomous vehicles. Trains and shuttles operate in controlled environments that can be monitored, and thus autonomous trains and shuttles can be deployed relatively easier than the other vehicles.

Autonomous vessels or ships would be available sooner than autonomous cars and trucks.

Legal and infrastructure questions need to be answered in order for fully autonomous cars and trucks can be used on public roads. Should autonomous vehicles operate in the same lane with conventional driver-operated vehicles? Do the roads need to change? What new rules of engagement should be established? Who would be liable in the event of an accident caused by an autonomous vehicle? Cultural issues surrounding the concept of a driverless vehicle may need to be overcome. How will most people react to the sight of a car with no person behind the wheel? How should a human driver engage with and interpret the signals sent by an autonomous car? How should human drivers share the road with autonomous cars? Resolving such cultural, legal, and infrastructure issues will extend the timeline in which autonomous cars and trucks become available for practical use.

The construction sector would be the last industry to automate. More technical development is required for this sector. Collaborative robots and mobile robots still need to be developed for several specialized occupations such as electrician and plumbing. Robots that have already been developed cover just a few occupations. More robots would be available in 8–15 years. Further development of autonomous vehicles operating in a swarm would be available in 25 years. While 3D printing might be available for one-room houses and other small-scale construction earlier on the timeline, 3D printing of large-scale buildings would take the entire timeline to become available. Legal issues would need to be resolved in order for 3D printing of large-scale buildings to commence.

11.5 Leading Industry Sectors

To recap, the administrative and support sector would be the first industry to automate. This makes logical sense, since most work relates to writing and organizing documents. There would be practically no external factors to slow down movement toward adopting new technological systems. Cost may be an issue for some organizations, but it could be easily overcome with a deeper analysis of the organization's budget. Organizations would be able to find areas in the budget that can be reduced and modified to invest in the new systems.

The educational services sector would be the second leader to automate. Although technological systems would not eliminate teachers, new systems would enable teachers to be more effective in their key role as an educator. Teachers will have more time to work with and motivate students. With course preparation and administration done by the systems, teachers can focus on teaching – not on administrative work.

What makes the administrative and support sector and the educational services sector easier and faster to automate is the software-based systems. The cost of implementation would be lower than that of hardware-based systems. Organizations would not need to invest in complicated hardware systems as compared to other industries.

11.6 Lagging Industry Sectors

The construction and transportation sectors would be the laggards in adopting technological systems for automation. The longer timeline would be driven by external factors that are beyond the control of technical development. Legal and infrastructure issues related to safety and liability need to resolved. Cultural factors on how the public will perceive the new systems need to be understood. Because these two industries have hardware-based systems, the cost of implementation can be very high. Complete modes of transportation whether by train, car, truck, or ship will require changes to existing vehicles and infrastructure. That would require budgetary changes for a number of organizations involved (e.g., government, public transit, and private industry). Construction companies will have to weigh the costs and benefits of using robots instead of human workers to do a variety of construction tasks. Labor unions that work on behalf of specialized construction workers will need to agree on the use of construction robots.

11.7 Conclusion of Business Automation Across All Eight Industry Sectors

Based on the timeline described above, business automation will be staggered across the eight industry sectors. All sectors would not automate at the same time. Because of availability, maturity, cost, adoption, and external factors surrounding the technological systems, some industries can move faster than others. Within a particular industry, large-sized organizations would adopt new systems more readily than small-sized organizations.

The unevenness of automation across industries creates a complicated situation for workers who would be replaced by machines. The next chapter will examine the situation closely. But workers will have to think carefully on where their next career move should be. A misstep might require a worker to have to make another career change. In the event of a mass layoff in one industry, would another industry be able to absorb that influx of laid-off workers?

The unevenness of automation would be a better outcome than to have all sectors automate at once. In the case where all sectors automate at the same time, workers displaced by automation will not have another industry to move to. In the unevenness situation, there can be another industry that can accept new workers so long as the new workers have similar skills and abilities that can be applied in the new industry.

Chapter 12

The Effect of Automation on the Labor Force

12.1 Chapter Summary

Chapter 12 describes the effect that automation will have on the labor force, summarizing all of the lost jobs and all of the new jobs identified in Chapters 3–10. The differences between the new jobs and the lost jobs are analyzed to identify the skills and abilities that human workers will need to transition to new occupations. General tips are provided to help workers to prepare themselves through additional education or training. Given what has been explained in previous chapters, the production equation is revisited to explain the use of the equation to find combinations of labor and machine inputs that would be optimal for a particular organization. The explanation of the production equation leads into a discussion of the implications that widespread automation across the economy could have for the labor force. The discussion touches upon economic issues that could create a dilemma for society. The chapter concludes with brief descriptions of next steps to examine the implications more fully in future studies.

12.2 Aggregation of Lost Jobs

Using 2019 total employment as a baseline, the total number of workers could fall by a quarter percent to less than 63.3 million across eight industry sectors. The number of workers displaced by business automation could be

DOI: 10.4324/9781003189329-13

21.3 million. This reduction in labor could save more than $2.8 billion per day on personnel expenditures, based on an average hourly wage of $18.97 with workers being paid as low as $12.42 per hour to as high as $33.46 per hour.

The agriculture sector would lead all industry sectors with a 63.8 percent decrease of its workforce. The accommodation and food services sector could follow shortly behind with a 61.5 percent decrease of its workforce. The administrative and support sector could see a loss of 36 percent of its workforce. The transportation sector and the manufacturing sector could have a decrease in workers by 27.3 percent and 24.1 percent, respectively. The construction sector could have its workforce fall by one-fifth. The educational services sector and the health care sector could have the smallest decrease in workers by 10.7 percent and 6.2 percent, respectively.

Figure 12.1 shows the number of workers displaced by business automation relative to 2019 total employment in the United States, broken down by

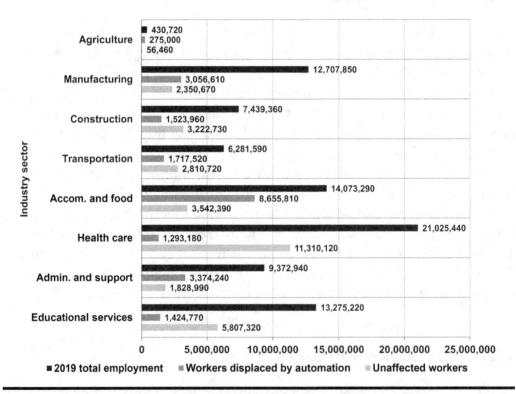

Figure 12.1 Comparison of displaced workers and unaffected workers.

Source: Author's analysis based on 2019 survey data from the Bureau of Labor Statistics.

industry sector. The chart also shows the number of workers unaffected by business automation by industry sector. The numbers for displaced workers and unaffected workers can be compared against each other and against the baseline 2019 total employment numbers.

Sixty-one (61) occupations could be lost across eight industry sectors. The accommodation and food services sector could potentially have the highest number of eliminated occupations followed by the administrative and support, manufacturing, and transportation sectors. Common jobs involved in the lost occupations would be those where workers carry, move, handle, or manipulate products and materials by hand. Jobs that would be replaced by machines would be those that require simple calculation and sorting of items, which lead to a predictable result. Other jobs that would be replaced by machines would be those that entail communicating with customers at a basic level such as saying hello or other greeting, directing someone to go a specific location, and offering a choice of specific items. Jobs that require entering information in a computer and handling and processing documents would be replaced by machines. All of these jobs replaced by machines would be jobs taken away from workers.

12.3 Aggregation of New Jobs

While occupations would be lost, there would be occupations that can be retained or elevated to a higher profile. More than 36 percent of the 2019 total employment of workers would be unaffected by business automation. The total number of retained workers would be 30.9 million. This new level of labor would cost $6.98 billion per day in personnel expenditures, based on an average hourly wage of $26.44 with workers earning as low as $17.79 per hour to as high as $34.26 per hour. These unaffected occupations earn higher wages on average in comparison to the lost occupations.

The health care sector would be able to retain the highest number of workers by as much as 53.8 percent. The transportation, educational services, and construction sectors could retain a high proportion of workers (44.7 percent, 43.7 percent, and 43.3 percent, respectively), assuming drivers, teachers, and highly specialized construction occupations are not eliminated. The accommodation and food services sector would be able to keep a quarter percent of staff. The administrative and support, manufacturing, and agriculture sectors would be able to retain a low proportion of workers (19.5 percent, 18.5 percent, and 13.1 percent, respectively).

Ninety (90) occupations could be retained across eight industry sectors with health care and educational services retaining the most occupations. The health care and educational services sectors have highly specialized occupations that require higher levels of education and training and in some cases certifications and licenses. Health- and education-related jobs require workers to have extensive and sophisticated conversations with individuals. Such complex forms of communication would not be available in the technological systems that can replace human workers. Doctors and nurses, for instance, have to communicate with patients in a manner that provides comfort and support. Teachers have to communicate with students in a manner that allows students to understand new lessons and concepts.

Common jobs that require autonomous vehicles and machines to be fully functional would require human workers. These jobs refer to the maintenance, repair, and management of technological systems. Workers will need to be mechanically inclined in order to diagnose a technical problem and to fix or change system parts. Workers would load and unload the machines with certain materials and start and stop operation of the machines. The role of the human operator will change from having full control of a machine to playing a support role where the human monitors operation and intervenes when needed.

Certain types of jobs will leverage the capabilities of both the machine and the human, so that work can be carried out more efficiently. An inspection machine, for example, would relieve an inspector from carrying out most of the procedural steps to inspect a product, allowing for a larger sample of products to be inspected. The inspector would then focus on analyzing the results of the sampled products and deciding to accept or reject the sampled products. In another example, a cooking robot would be capable of carrying out the steps to cook a particular dish. A restaurant cook would assist the robot by loading food ingredients, monitoring the robot's performance, unloading the cooked food onto a plate, and completing the plate with final touches.

Another new job will shift the role of first-line supervisors across most of the industry sectors. Rather than supervising workers, the first-line supervisors will oversee operation of machines. A number of workers would still be supervised but not in large number as before. A first-line supervisor may be responsible for starting, stopping, loading, unloading, monitoring, and repairing the machines or may delegate these tasks to machine operators.

12.4 Differences in Skills and Abilities

A worker will have to acquire new skills and develop new abilities in order to transition from a lost job to a new job. The skills and abilities of past jobs stand in contrast to the skills and abilities of future jobs. In past jobs, a worker needed to have the ability to lift and carry heavy loads or the ability to handle and manipulate small delicate items. A worker needed to have a number of basic skills for eye-hand coordination, simple math calculation, data entry, and basic communication. While tools and machines would have been used, a worker relied on his physical strength or mental capacity to take full advantage of the tools and machines. A worker maintained full control on the use of past technological systems and was a key driver in producing output.

The role switches completely around with a computerized machine doing the physical lifting or intensive computation. This then frees up an amount of time for a worker to focus on other tasks. These other tasks would fill in gaps or augment capabilities that a machine otherwise cannot do and that would be more effectively performed by a worker. A worker may no longer have full control to produce output but will have *partial control* to guide a machine to produce quality output.

The use of a future technological system will require a number of skills and abilities that raises a worker's capacity to think and reason and have patience. A worker will need to have a skill to understand how the internal parts of a machine operates. When a machine breaks down, she will have to troubleshoot the problem and get the machine back to work again. Part of the troubleshooting skill depends on the ability to read and interpret technical documents. A machine would come with schematics and diagrams that illustrate how the machine works. The worker then will need to know how to read the diagrams to identify where the source of the problem could be.

A computerized machine would have data involved either to input a set of data records or to output a report. A worker in this case will need to have a skill in data analysis to prepare data records and to review a data file.

A machine may output information or indicate a signal, and a worker would need to follow up on the information or signal by making a decision. A worker then will need to have a level of decision-making skill that allows her to make a sound decision based on the displayed information or signal.

A machine may take a certain length of time to complete a process, and a worker may be required to wait for the process to be completed. This will require the worker to have a degree of patience. The worker will need to have the ability to monitor a machine while it executes a procedure for a certain length of time.

A worker will need to feel comfortable interacting with a machine or robot, which can be viewed as an alien creature from a different culture. Similar to how people from different ethnicities and national origins have to learn to work together, a human worker needs to have the ability to work with a robot.

The new skills and abilities can be learned. Fundamental lessons of logic and critical thinking will be required. Through practical hands-on training, a worker can learn to interpret technical documents, troubleshoot mechanical failures, analyze data records, and make sound decisions. Learning to have patience and to work with a robot would require a longer time frame that ideally should begin at a young age in childhood. A person can become acclimated to working with a computerized machine after being exposed to it for a long period of time.

Workers who can master the new skills and abilities will be able to transition successfully to a new economy that increasingly relies on the future technological systems.

12.5 Equipment and Labor: The Production Equation Revisited

The business manager will need to determine how many workers should be employed and how many machines should be used in order to produce a certain quantity of goods or services. Chapter 1 explains an equation to calculate labor, equipment, and other resources that will produce an organization's goods or services. The business manager can use this mathematical formula to create several operating scenarios that show different combinations of humans and machines. One scenario would show the total cost of operations to have only humans and no machines. Another scenario would show the total cost of operations to have only machines and no humans. Other scenarios would show varied numbers of humans and machines in mixed combinations. Each mixed combination will have a different total cost of operations. The business manager can then decide which scenario would produce the total number of goods or services at the lowest cost.

There is no right or wrong answer to decide which operating scenario should be pursued. This is very subjective that depends on the context of a particular business. The industry sector that the business is in is a factor. The size of the organization is another factor. The type and quantity of product that will be produced factor in the decision-making process. The business manager would consider these other factors in addition to the calculated cost.

For any organization that has a choice between humans and machines, the following three questions need to be asked:

1. Will an All-Human Labor Force adequately meet the organization's needs and allow the organization to be profitable in the long run?
2. Will an All-Machine Equipment Force adequately meet the organization's needs and allow the organization to be profitable in the long run?
3. Will a Mix Labor–Equipment Force adequately meet the organization's needs and allow the organization to be profitable in the long run?

An affirmative answer to any one of the three foregoing questions will determine the operating scenario to pursue. If two or three of the questions result in affirmative answers, then the business manager will have to make a value judgment on which operating scenario should be pursued. In this case, the organization may be better off by *not* eliminating human workers.

A particular scenario that likely may not be viable is one that retains 100 percent of existing staff and adds new machines. This would mean no employees are laid off. As such, the organization would be increasing its total cost by the amount of machines that will be added.

In any operating scenario, there will be trade-offs to consider between the number of workers and the number of machines. Should there be more workers than machines or more machines than workers? Answering this question can be done by reviewing productivity metrics (e.g., cost per unit of output and output per unit of input). A scenario with a low cost per output and a high output per input would be viable. A scenario with a high cost per output and a low output per input would not be viable. An analysis of productivity metrics will identify the combination of workers, machines, and other resources that would be optimal for a particular organization. The end result will be the right balance of different resources.

12.6 Implications for the Labor Force

The data in Figure 12.1 show what would happen when organizations in all eight industry sectors adopt technological systems. This could occur in a little over a decade from now. The forecast reveals an alarming situation that is a cause for concern. What will 25.2 percent of the U.S. labor force do when they lose their jobs due to business automation?

The previous chapters highlight that those laid-off employees could move to another industry sector. This is a possibility when a few sectors reduce their workforce. But this may not be possible when *all* sectors reduce their workforce. When all sectors cut staff from payrolls, no industry will want to add new employees.

An option would be to have an industry sector rehire its own previously laid-off workers. The health care sector, for instance, may be able to move its 1.2 million displaced workers to its unaffected occupations. The educational services sector may be able to move its 1.4 million displaced workers to its unaffected occupations. In both instances, the displaced workers will have to obtain additional education or training. For the health care sector, displaced workers would train to become doctors, nurses, or medical technicians. For the educational services sector, displaced workers would train to become teachers. In both sectors, the displaced workers would be temporarily unemployed for about 1 or 2 years while they go through training.

The other industries may not be able to rehire displaced workers back into their sector. Even if they could, the additional numbers in higher wage occupations may be neither profitable nor optimal. Some organizations may see a considerable increase in their total cost of operations. An option in this case may be to enlarge the size of the pie by allowing more companies to form and enter the market. Newly established firms (e.g., start-ups led by entrepreneurs) could find funding and hire the displaced workers.

Accommodation and food services and administrative and support are two sectors of concern. These two industries have a large difference between their displaced workers and unaffected workers – with more of the former than of the latter. Organizations would likely not be able to rehire the displaced workers.

Displaced workers could obtain additional education or training and move to another industry. But the window of opportunity would be short. Workers will need to decide their future occupation, obtain required training, and find their new occupation in a short period of time. Within 10 years, four out of eight industry sectors may have adopted technological systems and begun to reduce their workforce. All of the earlier and recent displaced workers will be competing for limited job positions. A proportion of displaced workers could be unsuccessful and could become permanently unemployed.

Natural attrition would occur, allowing displaced workers to find vacancies left by persons who had retired or passed away. This bright spot, however, would not lead to large-scale vacancies equivalent to the scale of mass layoffs. Displaced workers could be waiting indefinitely for current employees to retire. Unless a policy exists to compel early retirement, attrition will occur gradually over time.

Advancements in health care is a factor that can extend the rate of attrition long into the future. Because of improved health and availability of medicines, persons are able to live longer and can potentially work beyond the age of 65. Thus, natural attrition may not be an option that solves the dilemma of displaced workers.

In sum, the impact of business automation on the labor force looks bleak when all eight industry sectors are automated. The impact could be less pronounced when all sectors do not automate at once. Displaced workers in early leaders of business automation could find new employment in other industries that have yet to automate. As more sectors automate, however, an increasing number of displaced workers will be competing for limited job openings. There could still be millions of people who may end up permanently unemployed when all sectors eventually reach full automation.

A group of permanent unemployed persons creates a dilemma for a society that depends on a consumer-driven economic system. How will persons survive? Without a job, a person cannot earn income. Without income, a person cannot buy and consume food and other products necessary to live. The inability to buy goods extends to the inability to pay rent for housing. Without housing, a person becomes homeless. Without these persons who otherwise would be consumers if they had a job and income, producers of manufactured goods will have a smaller percentage of the population who can be marketed and sold to. This market share of consumers would progressively decrease as more workers become displaced by automation and cannot find new occupations. The decreasing share of consumers could then reduce the amount of revenues that producers earn from the sale of their products. Without revenues, producers will have to reduce costs and eliminate staff. This then could lead to a collapse of the whole cycle of producers producing goods and consumers consuming goods.

12.7 Next Steps for Future Study

Further research needs to be done on developing specific case studies of various automation and labor scenarios across the eight industry sectors. Research needs to include collecting human resource and financial data from numerous organizations. The data would be used in the production equation to analyze total production with and without technological systems. The examination of production will look at organizations individually and in the aggregate.

Research on re-employment strategies needs to be done. This research will examine the ways in which workers displaced by automation can use to return to the labor force. Research needs to include an analysis of how long a person would need to be temporarily unemployed while he is in training for a new occupation.

Public policies need to be examined to find appropriate and cost-effective interventions to assist workers displaced by automation. Universal basic income needs to be explored, calculating how much should be disbursed to each person and how long disbursements should last. Various social welfare programs need to be examined, which includes the possible restructuring of existing programs. Research needs to include an examination of whether government agencies can sustainably fund such welfare programs.

Exploration of a new economic system needs to be carried out. What other system could replace the current consumer-driven economy? A system based on leisure where all persons no longer work at all needs to be included in the research. In such a leisure-based system, how would goods and services be provided? How would a leisure-based economy even function? The research needs to examine and re-examine all economic systems from the past and present. Development of completely novel programs and approaches needs to be explored.

Bibliography

Introduction

Acemoglu, Daron, and Pascual Restrepo. 2017. "Robots and Jobs: Evidence from US Labor Markets." NBER Working Paper No. 23285, March 2017. *National Bureau of Economic Research*. <www.nber.org/papers/w23285>. (Accessed 4 April 2020).

Engelman, Ryan. "The Second Industrial Revolution, 1870–1914." *U.S. History Scene*. <https://ushistoryscene.com/article/second-industrial-revolution/>. (Accessed 4 April 2020).

Floridi, Luciano. 2014. "Technological Unemployment, Leisure Occupation, and the Human Project." (6 May 2014), *Philosophy and Technology*, 27: 143–150. <https://doi.org/10.1007/s13347-014-0166-7>.

National Academies of Sciences, Engineering, and Medicine. 2017. *The Fourth Industrial Revolution: Proceedings of a Workshop – in Brief*. Washington, DC: The National Academies Press. <https://doi.org/10.17226/24699>.

New World Encyclopedia Contributors. 2018. "Industrial Revolution." (3 March 2018), *New World Encyclopedia*. <www.newworldencyclopedia.org/p/index.php?title=Industrial_Revolution&oldid=1009448>. (Accessed 4 April 2020).

Philbeck, Thomas, and Nicholas Davis. 2019. "The Fourth Industrial Revolution: Shaping A New Era." (22 January 2019), *Journal of International Affairs*. <https://jia.sipa.columbia.edu/fourth-industrial-revolution-shaping-new-era>. (Accessed 26 March 2020).

Rifkin, Jeremy. 2011. *The Third Industrial Revolution: How Lateral Power is Transforming Energy, the Economy, and the World*. New York: Palgrave Macmillan.

Schwab, Klaus. 2016. "The Fourth Industrial Revolution: What it Means, How to Respond." (14 January 2016), *World Economic Forum*. <www.weforum.org/agenda/2016/01/the-fourth-industrial-revolution-what-it-means-and-how-to-respond/>. (Accessed 26 March 2020).

Toffler, Alvin. 1980. *The Third Wave*. New York: Bantam Books.

Xu, Min, Jeanne M. David, and Suk Hi Kim. 2018. "The Fourth Industrial Revolution: Opportunities and Challenges." (8 March 2018), *International Journal of Financial Research*, 9, no. 2: 90–95. <https://doi.org/10.5430/ijfr.v9n2p90>.

Chapter 1

Baptist, Simon, and Cameron Hepburn. 2013. "Intermediate Inputs and Economic Productivity." *Philosophical Transactions of the Royal Society A*, 371: 20110565. <http://doi.org/10.1098/rsta.2011.0565>.

Chew, W. Bruce. 1998. "No-Nonsense Guide to Measuring Productivity." (January 1998), *Harvard Business Review*. <https://hbr.org/1988/01/no-nonsense-guide-to-measuring-productivity>. (Accessed 22 November 2020).

Cobb, Charles W., and Paul H. Douglas. 1928. "A Theory of Production." *The American Economic Review*, 18, no. 1: 139–165. <www.jstor.org/stable/1811556>.

Felipe, Jesus, and John McCombie. 2019. "The Illusions of Calculating Total Factor Productivity and Testing Growth Models: From Cobb-Douglas to Solow and Romer." ADB Economics Working Paper No. 596, October 2019. *Asian Development Bank*. <www.adb.org/sites/default/files/publication/534761/ewp-596-tfp-testing-growth-models.pdf>. (Accessed 22 November 2020).

Hellerstein, Judith K., and David Neumark. 2007. "Production Function and Wage Equation Estimation with Heterogeneous Labor: Evidence from a New Matched Employer-Employee Data Set." In *Hard-to-Measure Goods and Services: Essays in Honor of Zvi Griliches*, October 2007. Chicago: University of Chicago Press.

Jones, Charles I. 2019. "Paul Romer: Ideas, Nonrivalry, and Endogenous Growth." *The Scandinavian Journal of Economics*, 121, no. 3: 859–883. <https://web.stanford.edu/~chadj/RomerNobel.pdf>.

Romer, Paul M. 1989. "Endogenous Technological Change." NBER Working Paper No. 3210, December 1989. *National Bureau of Economic Research*. <www.nber.org/system/files/working_papers/w3210/w3210.pdf>. (Accessed 22 November 2020).

Solow, Robert M. 1957. "Technical Change and the Aggregate Production Function." *The Review of Economics and Statistics*, 39, no. 3: 312–320. <www.jstor.org/stable/1926047>.

Chapter 2

Ananthaswamy, Anil. 2020. "Physicists Create City-Sized Ultrasecure Quantum Network: Capable of Connecting Eight or More Users across Distances of 17 Kilometers, the Demonstration is another Milestone toward Developing a Fully Quantum Internet." (3 September 2020), *Scientific American*. <www.scientificamerican.com/article/physicists-create-city-sized-ultrasecure-quantum-network1/>. (Accessed 4 October 2020).

BBC News. 2019. "First Image of Einstein's 'Spooky' Particle Entanglement." (13 July 2019), *BBC*. <www.bbc.com/news/uk-scotland-glasgow-west-48971538>. (Accessed 6 November 2021).

Benenson, Yaakov et al. 2003. "DNA Molecule Provides a Computing Machine with Both Data and Fuel." (4 March 2003), *PNAS, Proceedings of the National Academy of Sciences of the United States of America*, 100, no. 5: 2191–2196. <https://doi.org/10.1073/pnas.0535624100>.

Bhatt, Ashutosh. 2011. "Sensors: Different Types of Sensors." (23 February 2011), *Engineers Garage*. <www.engineersgarage.com/article_page/sensors-different-types-of-sensors/>. (Accessed 18 July 2020).

Boyle, Alan. 2019. "Quantum Bits: Intel Unveils 'Horse Ridge,' a Cryogenic Chip for Quantum Computers." (9 December 2019), *GeekWire*. <www.geekwire.com/2019/quantum-bits-intel-unveils-horse-ridge-cryogenic-chip-quantum-computers/>. (Accessed 4 October 2020).

Brassard, Gilles et al. 1998. "Quantum Computing." (September 1998), *Proceedings of the National Academy of Sciences of the United States of America*, 95, no. 19: 11032–11033. <https://doi.org/10.1073/pnas.95.19.11032>.

Bringsjord, Selmer, and Naveen Sundar Govindarajulu. 2018. "Artificial Intelligence." (12 July 2018), *The Stanford Encyclopedia of Philosophy*. <https://plato.stanford.edu/entries/artificial-intelligence/>. (Accessed 18 July 2020).

Brown, Alan S. 2011. "Mechatronics and the Role of Engineers." (12 August 2011), *ASME*. <www.asme.org/topics-resources/content/mechatronics-and-the-role-of-engineers>. (Accessed 18 July 2020).

Bzdok, Danilo, Martin Krzywinski, and Naomi Altman. 2017. "Machine Learning: A Primer." (30 November 2017), *Nature Methods*, 14, no. 12: 1119–1120. <https://doi.org/10.1038/nmeth.4526>.

Cho, Adrian. 2020. "The Biggest Flipping Challenge in Quantum Computing." (9 July 2020), *Science*. <www.sciencemag.org/news/2020/07/biggest-flipping-challenge-quantum-computing>. (Accessed 4 October 2020).

Choi, Charles Q. 2020. "First Photonic Quantum Computer on the Cloud: Toronto-based Xanadu Suggests Its System Could Scale Up to Millions of Qubits." (9 September 2020), *IEEE Spectrum*. <https://spectrum.ieee.org/tech-talk/computing/hardware/photonic-quantum>. (Accessed 4 October 2020).

Crane, Leah. 2020. "Record-breaking Quantum Memory Brings Quantum Internet One Step Closer." (12 February 2020), *New Scientist*. <www.newscientist.com/article/2233317-record-breaking-quantum-memory-brings-quantum-internet-one-step-closer/>. (Accessed 4 October 2020).

Davenport, Thomas H., and Rajeev Ronanki. 2018. "Artificial Intelligence for the Real World." (January–February 2018), *Harvard Business Review*. <https://hbr.org/2018/01/artificial-intelligence-for-the-real-world>. (Accessed 18 July 2020).

de La Fuente, Jesus. "Properties of Graphene." *Graphenea*. <www.graphenea.com/pages/graphene-properties>. (Accessed 4 July 2021).

de Novato, Adrian. 2020. "Self-powered Alarm Fights Forest Fires, Monitors Environment." (24 June 2020), *MSU Today*. <https://msutoday.msu.edu/news/2020/self-powered-alarm-fights-forest-fires-monitors-environment>. (Accessed 18 July 2020). Link to full article <https://onlinelibrary.wiley.com/doi/10.1002/adfm.202003598>.

Di Paolo Emilio, Maurizio. 2020. "Quantum Computing is a Challenge for Cryptography." (10 February 2020), *EE Times*. <www.eetimes.com/quantum-computing-is-a-challenge-for-cryptography/#>. (Accessed 4 October 2020).

Dodabalapur, Ananth. 2006. "Organic and Polymer Transistors for Electronics." (April 2006), *Materials Today*, 9, no. 4: 24–30. <https://doi.org/10.1016/S1369-7021(06)71444-4>.

Donoho, David. 2017. "50 Years of Data Science." (19 December 2017), *Journal of Computational and Graphical Statistics*, 26, no. 4: 745–766, <https://doi.org/10.1080/10618600.2017.1384734>.

Du, Mengnan, Ninghao Liu, and Xia Hu. 2020. "Techniques for Interpretable Machine Learning." (January 2020), *Communications of the ACM*, 63, no. 1: 68–77. <https://cacm.acm.org/magazines/2020/1/241703-techniques-for-interpretable-machine-learning/fulltext>.

Dyer, Ezra. 2017. "Why Carbon Fiber Is the Miracle Material: Carbon Fiber Improves Everything. So Why Aren't We Making All Our Cars Out of It? We Went to Lamborghini's Factory to Find Out." (10 February 2017), *Popular Mechanics*. <www.popularmechanics.com/cars/car-technology/a25131/carbon-fiber-miracle-material/>. (Accessed 21 March 2020).

Dynes, J. F. et al. 2019. "Cambridge Quantum Network." (2019), *npj Quantum Information*, 5: 101. <https://doi.org/10.1038/s41534-019-0221-4>.

Eglowstein, Howard. 2020. "Introduction to Servo Motors." *Science Buddies*. <www.sciencebuddies.org/science-fair-projects/references/introduction-to-servo-motors>. (Accessed 18 July 2020).

Elbaz, Johann et al. 2013. "Powering the Programmed Nanostructure and Function of Gold Nanoparticles with Catenated DNA Machines." (13 June 2013), *Nature Communications*, 4. <https://doi.org/10.1038/ncomms3000>.

Endo, Masayuki, and Hiroshi Sugiyama. 2018. "DNA Origami Nanomachines." (18 July 2018), *Molecules*, 23, no. 7. <https://dol.org/10.3390/molecules23071766>.

Feast, Josh. 2019. "4 Ways to Address Gender Bias in AI." (20 November 2019), *Harvard Business Review*. <https://hbr.org/2019/11/4-ways-to-address-gender-bias-in-ai>. (Accessed 18 July 2020).

Ferguson, John E., and A. David Redish. 2011. "Wireless Communication with Implanted Medical Devices Using the Conductive Properties of the Body." (July 2011), *Expert Review of Medical Devices*, 8, no. 4: 427–433. <https://doi.org/10.1586/erd.11.16>.

Ge, Shanhai et al. 2020. "A New Approach to Both High Safety and High Performance of Lithium-ion Batteries." (28 February 2020), *Science Advances*, 6, no. 9. <https://advances.sciencemag.org/content/6/9/eaay7633>.

Gibbs, Samuel. 2015. "Moore's Law Wins: New Chips Have Circuits 10,000 Times Thinner Than Hairs." (9 July 2015), *The Guardian*. <www.theguardian.com/technology/2015/jul/09/moores-law-new-chips-ibm-7nm>. (Accessed 4 July 2021).

Gibney, Elizabeth. 2017. "Magnetic Hard Drives Go Atomic: Physicists Demonstrate the First Single-atom Magnetic Storage." (8 March 2017), *Nature*. <www.nature.com/news/magnetic-hard-drives-go-atomic-1.21599>. (Accessed 4 October 2020).

Giles, Martin. 2019. "Explainer: What is a Quantum Computer? How it Works, Why It's So Powerful, and Where It's Likely to Be Most Useful First." (29 January 2019), *MIT Technology Review*. <www.technologyreview.com/2019/01/29/66141/what-is-quantum-computing/>. (Accessed 4 October 2020).

Giovannetti, Vittorio, Seth Lloyd, and Lorenzo Maccone. 2008. "Quantum Random Access Memory." (21 April 2008), *Physical Review Letters*, 100, no. 16. <https://doi.org/10.1103/PhysRevLett.100.160501>.

Han, Seungyong et al. 2018. "Battery-free, Wireless Sensors for Full-body Pressure and Temperature Mapping." (4 April 2018), *Science Translational Medicine*, <https://stm.sciencemag.org/content/10/435/eaan4950.full>.

Hannah, Stuart et al. 2018. "Multifunctional Sensor Based on Organic Field-effect Transistor and Ferroelectric Poly(vinylidene fluoride trifluoroethylene)." (30 January 2018), *Organic Electronics*, 56: 170–177 <https://doi.org/10.1016/j.orgel.2018.01.041>.

Hayes, Brian. 2014. "Delving into Deep Learning." (May–June 2014), *American Scientist*, 102, no. 3: 186. <https://doi.org/10.1511/2014.108.186>.

Herculano-Houzel, Suzana. 2009. "The Human Brain in Numbers: A Linearly Scaled-up Primate Brain." (9 November 2009), *Frontiers in Human Neuroscience*, 3, no. 31: 1–11. <https://doi.org/10.3389/neuro.09.031.2009>.

Herkewitz, William. 2016. "They Built the Single-Atom Engine And It Actually Works." (14 April 2016), *Popular Mechanics*. <www.popularmechanics.com/science/energy/a20406/single-atom-engine-works/>. (Accessed 21 March 2020).

Hicks, Stephanie C., and Roger D. Peng. 2019. "Elements and Principles of Data Analysis." (20 March 2019). <https://arxiv.org/abs/1903.07639v1>.

Hopkinson, Mark. 2015. "With Silicon Pushed to Its Limits, What Will Power the Next Electronics Revolution?" (27 August 2015), *Phys.org*. <https://phys.org/news/2015-08-silicon-limits-power-electronics-revolution.html>. (Accessed 3 July 2021).

Hu, Meng et al. 2013. "Compressed Carbon Nanotubes: A Family of New Multifunctional Carbon Allotropes." (25 February 2013), *Scientific Reports*, 3. <https://doi.org/10.1038/srep01331>.

Irving, Michael. 2019. "CRISPR Used to Build Dual-core Computers Inside Human Cells." (17 April 2019), *New Atlas*. <https://newatlas.com/crispr-cell-computer/59336/>. (Accessed 21 March 2020).

Jeewandara, Thamarasee. 2019. "Stretchable, Self-healing and Semiconducting Polymer Films for Electronic Skin (e-skin)." (15 November 2019). <https://phys.org/news/2019-11-stretchable-selfhealing-semiconducting-polymer-electronic.html>. (Accessed 21 March 2020).

Kim, Hyojin, Daniel Bojar, and Martin Fussenegger. 2019. "A CRISPR/Cas9-based Central Processing Unit to Program Complex Logic Computation in Human Cells." (9 April 2019), *PNAS*, 116, no. 15: 7214–7219. <https://doi.org/10.1073/pnas.1821740116>.

Kinloch, Ian A. et al. 2018. "Composites with Carbon Nanotubes and Graphene: An Outlook." (2 November 2018), *Science*, 362: 547–553. <https://science.sciencemag.org/content/362/6414/547.full>.

Kreupl, Franz. 2013. "The Carbon-nanotube Computer Has Arrived." (26 September 2013), *Nature*, 501: 495–496. <https://doi.org/10.1038/501495a>.

Lanzara, Alessandra. 2015. "Graphene Gets a Good Gap." (21 September 2015), *Physics*, 8, no. 91. <https://physics.aps.org/articles/v8/91>.

Lauback, Stephanie et al. 2018. "Real-time Magnetic Actuation of DNA Nanodevices via Modular Integration with Stiff Micro-levers." *Nature Communications*, 9. <https://doi.org/10.1038/s41467-018-03601-5>.

Lei, Ting et al. 2017. "Biocompatible and Totally Disintegrable Semiconducting Polymer for Ultrathin and Ultralightweight Transient Electronics." (16 May 2017), *PNAS*, 114, no. 20: 5107–5112. <https://doi.org/10.1073/pnas.1701478114>.

Lent, Roberto et al. 2011. "How Many Neurons Do You Have? Some Dogmas of Quantitative Neuroscience under Revision." (13 December 2011), *European Journal of Neuroscience*, 35, no. 1: 1–9. <https://doi.org/10.1111/j.1460-9568.2011.07923.x>.

Lewotsky, Kristin. 2007. "Serving Up Better Servos." (17 January 2007), *Motion Control Online*. <www.motioncontrolonline.org/content-detail.cfm/Motion-Control-Technical-Features/Serving-Up-Better-Servos/content_id/66>. (Accessed 18 July 2020).

Lewotsky, Kristin. 2007. "Servos Drive Automotive Manufacturing/Automation for Auto Motion." (24 September 2007), *Motion Control Online*. <www.motioncontrolonline.org/content-detail.cfm/Motion-Control-Technical-Features/Servos-Drive-Automotive-Manufacturing-Automation-for-Auto-Motion/content_id/1064>. (Accessed 18 July 2020).

Liu, Johan et al. 2013. "Carbon Nanotubes for Electronics Manufacturing and Packaging: From Growth to Integration." (13 March 2013), *Advanced Manufacturing*, 1: 13–27. <https://doi.org/10.1007/s40436-013-0007-4>.

Matulka, Rebecca. 2013. "Top 9 Things You Didn't Know about Carbon Fiber." (29 March 2013), *U.S. Department of Energy*. <www.energy.gov/articles/top-9-things-you-didn-t-know-about-carbon-fiber>. (Accessed 21 March 2020).

Merriam-Webster. "Data." *Merriam-Webster.com Dictionary*. <www.merriam-webster.com/dictionary/data>. (Accessed 31 October 2021).

Motion Control Online Marketing Team. 2019. "Servo Motors Explained and Why They're Useful in Robotics." (2 July 2019), *Motion Control Online*. <www.motioncontrolonline.org/blog-article.cfm/Servo-Motors-Explained-and-Why-They-re-Useful-in-Robotics/87>. (Accessed 18 July 2020).

Murata, Hiromasa et al. 2019. "High-Electrical-Conductivity Multilayer Graphene Formed by Layer Exchange with Controlled Thickness and Interlayer." (11 March 2019), *Scientific Reports*, 9. <https://doi.org/10.1038/s41598-019-40547-0>.

Namuduri, Srikanth et al. 2020. "Review – Deep Learning Methods for Sensor Based Predictive Maintenance and Future Perspectives for Electrochemical Sensors." (28 January 2020), *Journal of The Electrochemical Society*, 167, no. 3. <https://doi.org/10.1149/1945-7111/ab67a8>.

National Academy of Engineering. 2019. *Frontiers of Engineering: Reports on Leading-Edge Engineering from the 2018 Symposium*. Washington, DC: The National Academies Press. <https://doi.org/10.17226/25333>.

National Aeronautics and Space Administration. 2020. "Remote Sensors." *Earthdata*. <https://earthdata.nasa.gov/learn/remote-sensors>. (Accessed 18 July 2020).

National Institute of Biomedical Imaging and Bioengineering. 2016. "Sensors." (October 2016). <www.nibib.nih.gov/science-education/science-topics/sensors>. (Accessed 18 July 2020).

National Institute of Neurological Disorders and Stroke. 2019. "Brain Basics: The Life and Death of a Neuron." (16 December 2019) <www.ninds.nih.gov/Disorders/Patient-Caregiver-Education/Life-and-Death-Neuron>. (Accessed 18 July 2020).

New World Encyclopedia Contributors. 2019. "Abacus." (13 October 2019), *New World Encyclopedia*. <www.newworldencyclopedia.org/entry/abacus>. (Accessed 4 October 2020).

Pang, Xiao-Ling et al. 2020. "A Hybrid Quantum Memory – Enabled Network at Room Temperature." (7 February 2020), *Science Advances*, 6, no. 6. <https://doi.org/10.1126/sciadv.aax1425>.

Petersen, Philip, Grigory Tikhomirov, and Lulu Qian. 2018. "Information-based Autonomous Reconfiguration in Systems of Interacting DNA Nanostructures." *Nature Communications*, 9. <https://doi.org/10.1038/s41467-018-07805-7>.

Phys.org. 2018. "Built for Speed: DNA Nanomachines Take a (Rapid) Step Forward." (7 May 2018). <https://phys.org/news/2018-05-built-dna-nanomachines-rapid.html>. (Accessed 21 March 2020).

Phys.org. 2017. "How Carbon Nanotubes Could Be Used in Future Electronic Devices." (22 November 2017). <https://phys.org/news/2017-11-carbon-nanotubes-future-electronic-devices.html>. (Accessed 21 March 2020).

Phys.org. 2020. "IonQ Announces Development of Next-generation Quantum Computer." (2 October 2020). <https://phys.org/news/2020-10-ionq-next-generation-quantum.html>. (Accessed 4 October 2020).

Phys.org. 2020. "New Nano-engineering Strategy Shows Potential for Improved Advanced Energy Storage." (6 July 2020). <https://phys.org/news/2020-07-nano-engineering-strategy-potential-advanced-energy.html>. (Accessed 18 July 2020).

Phys.org. 2019. "New Research Unlocks Properties for Quantum Information Storage and Computing." (6 June 2019). <https://phys.org/news/2019-06-properties-quantum-storage.html>. (Accessed 4 October 2020).

Phys.org. 2020. "Physicists Develop World's Best Quantum Bits." (18 May 2020). <https://phys.org/news/2020-05-physicists-world-quantum-bits.html>. (Accessed 4 October 2020).

Phys.org. 2020. "Replacing Lithium with Sodium in Batteries." (17 July 2020). <https://phys.org/news/2020-07-lithium-sodium-batteries.html>. (Accessed 18 July 2020).

Phys.org. 2011. "Storing Quantum Information Permanently." (27 July 2011). <https://phys.org/news/2011-07-quantum-permanently.html>. (Accessed 4 October 2020).

Phys.org. 2019. "Stretchable, Self-healing and Semiconducting Polymer Films for Electronic Skin (e-skin)." (15 November 2019). <https://phys.org/news/2019-11-stretchable-self-healing-semiconducting-polymer-electronic.html>. (Accessed 21 March 2020).

Phys.org. 2015. "With Silicon Pushed to Its Limits, What Will Power the Next Electronics Revolution?" (27 August 2015). <https://phys.org/news/2015-08-silicon-limits-power-electronics-revolution.html>. (Accessed 3 July 2020).

Phys.org. 2004. "World's First Commercialization of Mercury-Free Silver Oxide Battery." (29 September 2004). <https://phys.org/news/2004-09-world-commercialization-mercury-free-silver-oxide.html>. (Accessed 18 July 2020).

Ryan, Ken. 2011. "Factory Automation: Mechatronics: A Vertical Perspective." (January/February 2011), *InTech Magazine*. <www.isa.org/standards-and-pub lications/isa-publications/intech-magazine/2011/february/factory-automation-mechatronics-a-vertical-perspective/>. (Accessed 18 July 2020).

Sang, Mingyu et al. 2019. "Electronic and Thermal Properties of Graphene and Recent Advances in Graphene Based Electronics Applications." (5 March 2019), *Nanomaterials*, 9, no. 3. <https://doi.org/10.3390/nano9030374>.

Santo, Brian. 2009. "25 Microchips That Shook the World: A List of Some of the Most Innovative, Intriguing, and Inspiring Integrated Circuits." (1 May 2009), *IEEE Spectrum*, <https://spectrum.ieee.org/tech-history/silicon-revolution/25-microchips-that-shook-the-world>.

Savage, Neil. 2020. "Google's Quantum Computer Achieves Chemistry Milestone: A Downsized Version of the Company's Sycamore Chip Performed a Record-breaking Simulation of a Chemical Reaction." (4 September 2020), *Scientific American*. <www.scientificamerican.com/article/googles-quantum-computer-achieves-chemistry-milestone/>. (Accessed 4 October 2020).

Sen, Tapas. 2016. "Meet the Nanomachines That Could Drive a Medical Revolution." (21 April 2016), *Singularity Hub*. <https://singularityhub.com/2016/04/21/meet-the-nanomachines-that-could-drive-a-medical-revolution/>. (Accessed 21 March 2020).

Silberzahn, R. et al. 2018. "Many Analysts, One Data Set: Making Transparent How Variations in Analytic Choices Affect Results." *Advances in Methods and Practices in Psychological Science*, 1, no. 3: 337–356. <https://doi.org/10.1177/2515245917747646>.

Sun, Han-Sheng, Yu-Cheng Chiu, and Wen-Chang Chen. 2017. "Renewable Polymeric Materials for Electronic Applications." *Polymer Journal*, 49: 61–73. <https://doi.org/10.1038/pj.2016.95>.

Sutton, Jane, and Zubin Austin. 2015. "Qualitative Research: Data Collection, Analysis, and Management." (May–June 2015), *The Canadian Journal of Hospital Pharmacy*, 68, no. 3: 226–231. <https://doi.org/10.4212/cjhp.v68i3.1456>.

Traverso, G. et al. 2015. "Physiologic Status Monitoring via the Gastrointestinal Tract." (18 November 2015), *PLoS ONE*, 10, no. 11. <https://doi.org/10.1371/journal.pone.0141666>.

Tukey, John W. 1961. "The Future of Data Analysis." Research sponsored by the U.S. Army Research Office, Contract DA36–034-ORD-2297 with Princeton University, 1 July 1961. *Princeton University and Bell Telephone Laboratories*. Preserved by the Institute of Mathematical Statistics and JSTOR.

Turing, A. M. 1950. "I. – Computing Machinery and Intelligence." (October 1950), *Mind*, LIX, no. 236: 433–460. <https://doi.org/10.1093/mind/LIX.236.433>.

Uechi, Edward Y. 2020. *Public Service Information Technology: The Definitive Manager's Guide to Harnessing Technology for Cost-Effective Operations and Services*. New York: Routledge/Productivity Press.

Uhl, Edgar, Peter Mayer, and Henry Dube. 2020. "Active and Unidirectional Acceleration of Biaryl Rotation by a Molecular Motor." (15 January 2020), *Angewandte Chemie International Edition*, 59: 5730–5737. <https://doi.org/10.1002/anie.201913798>.

Ulmer, Simone. 2004. "Storing Quantum Information Permanently." (27 July 2011). <https://phys.org/news/2011-07-quantum-permanently.html>. (Accessed 4 October 2020).

Wan, Sijie et al. 2018. "Sequentially Bridged Graphene Sheets with High Strength, Toughness, and Electrical Conductivity." (22 May 2018), *PNAS*, 115, no. 21: 5359–5364. <https://doi.org/10.1073/pnas.1719111115>.

Wenz, John. 2019. "Why This New 16-Bit Carbon Nanotube Processor Is Such a Big Deal: Scientists Just Created a Carbon Nanotube Chip, But What Are Carbon Nanotubes Exactly?" (28 August 2019), *Popular Mechanics*. <www.popularmechanics.com/technology/a28838017/what-are-ca>. (21 March 2020).

Wolchover, Natalie. 2020. "Artificial Intelligence Will Do What We Ask. That's a Problem." (30 January 2020), *Quanta Magazine*. <www.quantamagazine.org/artificial-intelligence-will-do-what-we-ask-thats-a-problem-20200130/>. (Accessed 18 July 2020).

Wolf, Lauren K. 2013. "The Nanotube Computer Has Arrived: Electronics: Carbon-based Alternative to Silicon Circuitry Runs Programs and Executes Instructions." (26 September 2013), *Chemical & Engineering News*. <https://cen.acs.org/articles/91/web/2013/09/Nanotube-Computer-Arrived.html>. (Accessed 4 July 2021).

Wolpert, Stuart. 2020. "Physicists Develop World's Best Quantum Bits." (18 May 2020). <https://phys.org/news/2020-05-physicists-world-quantum-bits.html>. (Accessed 4 October 2020).

Wu, Ruqian. 2018. "What's the Noise Eating Quantum Bits?" (6 January 2018), *U.S. Department of Energy, Office of Science*, <www.energy.gov/science/bes/articles/what-s-noise-eating-quantum-bits>. (Accessed 4 October 2020).

Xin, Ling et al. 2019. "A Rotary Plasmonic Nanoclock." *Nature Communications*, 10. <https://doi.org/10.1038/s41467-019-13444-3>.

Yang, Gao et al. 2018. "Structure of Graphene and Its Disorders: A Review." (29 August 2018), *Science and Technology of Advanced Materials*, 19, no. 1: 613–648. <https://doi.org/10.1080/14686996.2018.1494493>.

Yeomans, Mike. 2015. "What Every Manager Should Know About Machine Learning." (7 July 2015), *Harvard Business Review*. <https://hbr.org/2015/07/what-every-manager-should-know-about-machine-learning>. (Accessed 18 July 2020).

Zalba, M. Fernando Gonzalez et al. 2019. "Quantum Computing Using Silicon Transistors: From Bits to Quantum Bits." (2019), *Hitachi Review*. <www.hitachi.com/rev/archive/2019/r2019_04/04c03/index.html>. (Accessed 4 October 2020).

Zandonella, Catherine. 2019. "In Leap for Quantum Computing, Silicon Quantum Bits Establish a Long-distance Relationship." (30 December 2019), *Princeton University*. <www.princeton.edu/news/2019/12/30/leap-quantum-computing-silicon-quantum-bits-establish-long-distance-relationship>. (Accessed 4 October 2020).

Zhao, Jiangqi et al. 2019. "A Fully Integrated and Self-Powered Smartwatch for Continuous Sweat Glucose Monitoring." *ACS Sens. 2019*, 4, no. 7: 1925–1933. <https://pubs.acs.org/doi/abs/10.1021/acssensors.9b00891>.

Zhao, Qian et al. 2019. "Review on the Electrical Resistance/Conductivity of Carbon Fiber Reinforced Polymer." (11 June 2019), *Applied Sciences*, 9. <https://doi.org/10.3390/app9112390>.

Chapter 3

Anandan, Tanya M. 2019. "Cultivating Robotics and AI for Sustainable Agriculture." (22 July 2019), *Robotics Online*. <www.robotics.org/content-detail.cfm/Industrial-Robotics-Industry-Insights/Cultivating-Robotics-and-AI-for-Sustainable-Agriculture/content_id/8195>. (Accessed 9 January 2021).

Astill, Gregory, Agnes Perez, and Suzanne Thornsbury. 2020. "Developing Automation and Mechanization for Specialty Crops: A Review of U.S. Department of Agriculture Programs." Report to Congress, AP-082, February 2020. *U.S. Department of Agriculture, Economic Research Service*. <www.ers.usda.gov/webdocs/publications/95828/ap-082.pdf?v=5088.9>.

Bedord, Laurie. 2017. "How Automation Will Transform Farming." (29 November 2017), *Successful Farming*. <www.agriculture.com/technology/robotics/how-automation-will-transform-farming>. (Accessed 9 January 2021).

Bedord, Laurie. 2020. "Robots on the Rise: As Farmers Become More Comfortable with Automation, Companies Forge Ahead to Evolve 8 Concepts." (19 August 2020), *Successful Farming*. <www.agriculture.com/robots-on-the-rise>. (Accessed 9 January 2021).

Belton, Padraig. 2016. "In the Future, Will Farming Be Fully Automated?" (25 November 2016), *BBC*. <www.bbc.com/news/business-38089984>. (Accessed 9 January 2021).

Byrum, Joseph. 2018. "The Challenges for Artificial Intelligence in Agriculture." (24 April 2018), *Plug and Play*. <www.plugandplaytechcenter.com/resources/artificial-intelligence-agtech/>. (Accessed 9 January 2021).

Casey, Marcus, and Ember Smith. 2020. "Automation from Farm to Table: Technology's Impact on the Food Industry." (23 November 2020), *Brookings Institution*. <www.brookings.edu/blog/up-front/2020/11/23/automation-from-farm-to-table-technologys-impact-on-the-food-industry/>. (Accessed 9 January 2021).

Daniels, Jeff. 2018. "From Strawberries to Apples, a Wave of Agriculture Robotics May Ease the Farm Labor Crunch." (8 March 2018), *CNBC*. <www.cnbc.com/2018/03/08/wave-of-agriculture-robotics-holds-potential-to-ease-farm-labor-crunch.html>. (Accessed 9 January 2021).

Farm Collector Staff. 1983. "Lombard Steam Log Hauler." (1 March 1983), *Farm Collector*. <www.farmcollector.com/steam-traction/lombard-steam-log-hauler/>. (Accessed 19 November 2021).

Ganzel, Bill. "Agricultural Machinery during the 1940s." *Wessels Living History Farm*. <https://livinghistoryfarm.org/farminginthe40s/machines_03.html>. (Accessed 9 January 2021).

Ganzel, Bill. 2007. "Cotton Harvesting during the 1950s and 60s." *Wessels Living History Farm*. <https://livinghistoryfarm.org/farminginthe50s/machines_15.html>. (Accessed 9 January 2021).

Ganzel, Bill. "Cultivators on the Farm during the 1940s." *Wessels Living History Farm*. <https://livinghistoryfarm.org/farminginthe40s/machines_04.html>. (Accessed 9 January 2021).

Ganzel, Bill. 2007. "Farm Building Technology Goes from Barns to Behlen." *Wessels Living History Farm*. <https://livinghistoryfarm.org/farminginthe50s/machines_16.html>. (Accessed 9 January 2021).

Ganzel, Bill. 2006. "Farm Machinery during the 1950s." *Wessels Living History Farm*. <https://livinghistoryfarm.org/farminginthe50s/machines_01.html>. (Accessed 9 January 2021).

Ganzel, Bill. 2007. "Harvest Technology during the 1950s and 60s." *Wessels Living History Farm*. <https://livinghistoryfarm.org/farminginthe50s/machines_12.html>. (Accessed 9 January 2021).

Ganzel, Bill. 2007. "Harvesting Wheat during the 1950s and 60s." *Wessels Living History Farm*. <https://livinghistoryfarm.org/farminginthe50s/machines_14.html>. (Accessed 9 January 2021).

Ganzel, Bill. "Haying Equipment during the 1940s." *Wessels Living History Farm*. <https://livinghistoryfarm.org/farminginthe40s/machines_06.html>. (Accessed 9 January 2021).

Ganzel, Bill. "Horses Finally Lose their Jobs on the Farm during the 1940s." *Wessels Living History Farm*. <https://livinghistoryfarm.org/farminginthe40s/machines_13.html>. (Accessed 9 January 2021).

Ganzel, Bill. 2007. "Minimum Tillage Changes Planters & Cultivators." *Wessels Living History Farm.* <https://livinghistoryfarm.org/farminginthe50s/machines_11.html>. (Accessed 9 January 2021).

Ganzel, Bill. 2007. "Planter Technology during the 1950s and 60s." *Wessels Living History Farm.* <https://livinghistoryfarm.org/farminginthe50s/machines_10.html>. (Accessed 9 January 2021).

Ganzel, Bill. 2007. "Self-Propelled Corn Combines during the 1950s and 60s." *Wessels Living History Farm.* <https://livinghistoryfarm.org/farminginthe50s/machines_13.html>. (Accessed 9 January 2021).

Ganzel, Bill. "Tractor Innovations during the 1940s." *Wessels Living History Farm.* <https://livinghistoryfarm.org/farminginthe40s/machines_02.html>. (Accessed 9 January 2021).

Geller, Tom. 2016. "Farm Automation Gets Smarter." (November 2016), *Communications of the ACM*, 59, no. 11: 18–19. <https://cacm.acm.org/magazines/2016/11/209134-farm-automation-gets-smarter/fulltext#>.

Hau L. Lee et al. 2017. "Technology in Agribusiness: Opportunities to Drive Value." White Paper, August 2017. Stanford Value Chain Innovation Initiative. *Stanford University Graduate School of Business.*

Ku, Linly. 2019. "How Automation is Transforming the Farming Industry." (20 May 2019), *Plug and Play.* <www.plugandplaytechcenter.com/resources/how-automation-transforming-farming-industry/>. (Accessed 9 January 2021).

Moore, Sam. 1999. "Invention of the Crawler Tractor." (1 November 1999), *Farm Collector.* <www.farmcollector.com/company-history/invention-of-the-crawler-tractor/>. (Accessed 19 November 2021).

Mowitz, Dave. 2020. "Irrigation: Autonomous Pivots: Fully Automatic Irrigation Is a Reality." (23 November 2020), *Successful Farming.* <www.agriculture.com/technology/robotics/irrigation-autonomous-pivots>. (Accessed 9 January 2021).

National Academy of Engineering. "Agricultural Mechanization Timeline." *Greatest Engineering Achievements.* <www.greatachievements.org/?id=3725>. (Accessed 9 January 2021). Adapted from the book: Constable, George and Bob Somerville. 2003. *A Century of Innovation: Twenty Engineering Achievements That Transformed Our Lives.* Washington, DC: Joseph Henry Press.

O'Dell, Larry. "Agricultural Mechanization." *The Encyclopedia of Oklahoma History and Culture.* <www.okhistory.org/publications/enc/entry.php?entry=AG005>. (Accessed 9 January 2021).

Saiz-Rubio, Verónica, and Francisco Rovira-Más. 2020. "From Smart Farming towards Agriculture 5.0: A Review on Crop Data Management." (3 February 2020), *Agronomy*, 10, no. 2. <http://doi.org/10.3390/agronomy10020207>.

Schirmer, Julian et al. 2021. "Emerging Innovation Patterns in Digital Agriculture: A Study of 198 Digital Solutions from 116 Startups." Proceedings of the 54th Hawaii International Conference on System Sciences, 5 January 2021. *University of Hawaii, Hamilton Library.* <https://hdl.handle.net/10125/71227>.

Schlebecker, John T. 1972. *Agricultural Implements and Machines in the Collection of the National Museum of History and Technology*, Smithsonian Studies in History and Technology, No. 17.1972. Washington, DC: Smithsonian Institution Press.

Steward, Brian, Jingyao Gai, and Lie Tang. 2019. "The Use of Agricultural Robots in Weed Management and Control." In *Robotics and Automation for Improving Agriculture*, edited by John Billingsley. Burleigh Dodds Series in Agricultural Science. Cambridge, UK: Burleigh Dodds Science Publishing.

U.S. Bureau of Labor Statistics. 2021. "Industries at a Glance: Agriculture, Forestry, Fishing and Hunting: NAICS 11." (8 January 2021), *U.S. Department of Labor, Bureau of Labor Statistics*. <www.bls.gov/iag/tgs/iag11.htm>. (Accessed 10 January 2021).

Vincent, James. 2018. "The Robotic Farm of the Future Isn't What You'd Expect." (9 October 2018), *The Verge*. <www.theverge.com/2018/10/9/17950502/robot-farm-future-iron-ox-agriculture-automation>. (Accessed 9 January 2021).

Wincent. 2016. "iSow and iReap – The Automation and Digitization of Farming." (18 November 2016), *Harvard Business School, Digital Initiative*. <https://digital.hbs.edu/platform-rctom/submission/isow-and-ireap-the-automation-and-digitization-of-farming/#>. (Accessed 9 January 2021).

Chapter 4

Adams, Matt, Glenn Snyder, and Matt Szuhaj. 2012. "The Automation Evolution: How I Learned to Stop Worrying and Love the Future of Manufacturing." *Deloitte Review*, no. 11. <https://www2.deloitte.com/us/en/insights/deloitte-review/issue-11/the-automation-evolution-in-manufacturing.html>

Atack, Jeremy, Robert A. Margo, and Paul W. Rhode. 2019. "'Automation' of Manufacturing in the Late Nineteenth Century: The Hand and Machine Labor Study." (Spring 2019), *Journal of Economic Perspectives*, 33, no. 2: 51–70. <https://doi.org/10.1257/jep.33.2.51>.

Boisset, Fabrice. 2018. "The History of Industrial Automation in Manufacturing." (25 May 2018), *Motion Control Online*. <www.motioncontrolonline.org/content-detail.cfm/Motion-Control-News/The-History-of-Industrial-Automation-in-Manufacturing/content_id/2570>. (Accessed 9 January 2021).

CB Insights. 2019. "Future Factory: How Technology Is Transforming Manufacturing." (27 June 2019), *CB Insights*. <www.cbinsights.com/research/future-factory-manufacturing-tech-trends/>. (Accessed 9 January 2021).

Corday, Robert. 2014. "The Evolution of Assembly Lines: A Brief History." (24 April 2014), *Robohub*. <https://robohub.org/the-evolution-of-assembly-lines-a-brief-history/>. (Accessed 9 January 2021).

Devereaux, Doug. 2019. "5 Manufacturing Technology Trends to Watch in 2019." (7 February 2019), *Manufacturing Innovation Blog, Manufacturing Extension Partnership*. U.S. Department of Commerce, National Institute of Standards and Technology. <www.nist.gov/blogs/manufacturing-innovation-blog/5-manufacturing-technology-trends-watch-2019-0>. (Accessed 9 January 2021).

Giffi, Craig et al. 2018. "2018 Deloitte and The Manufacturing Institute Skills Gap and Future of Work Study." *Deloitte Insights*. <https://www2.deloitte.com/us/en/pages/manufacturing/articles/future-of-manufacturing-skills-gap-study.html>.

Guizzo Erico. 2011. "ABB's FRIDA Offers Glimpse of Future Factory Robots." (19 April 2011), *IEEE Spectrum*. <https://spectrum.ieee.org/abb-factory-robot-frida>. (Accessed 21 November 2021).

Hayden, Ernie. 2015. "An Abbreviated History of Automation and Industrial Controls System and Cybersecurity." Global Information Assurance Certification Paper, 22 January 2015. *SANS Institute*. <www.giac.org/paper/gicsp/95/abbreviated-history-automation-industrial-controls-system-cybersecurity/139645>.

History.com Editors. 2018. "Interchangeable Parts." (21 August 2018), *History*. <www.history.com/topics/inventions/interchangeable-parts>. (Accessed 20 November 2021).

Lewis, Chris. 2017. "New Robotics Impact the Future of Distribution." (15 August 2017), *Food Logistics*. <www.foodlogistics.com/software-technology/article/12354811/new-robotics-impact-the-future-of-distribution>. (Accessed 9 January 2021).

Matrix. 2011. "CAT in Major Autonomous Truck Milestone with Fortescue Deal . . . while Rio Doubles its Komatsu Driverless Fleet." (6 July 2011), *International Mining*. <https://im-mining.com/2011/07/06/cat-in-major-autonomous-truck-milestone-with-fortescue-dealwhile-rio-doubles-its-komatsu-driverless-fleet/>. (Accessed 20 November 2021).

Overstreet, Kim. 2020. "Is Wide-Spread Use of AI and Machine Intelligence in Manufacturing Still Years Away?" (18 September 2020), *OEM*. <www.oemmagazine.org/home/article/21194788/is-widespread-use-of-ai-machine-intelligence-in-manufacturing-still-years-away>. (Accessed 9 January 2021).

Singh, Rajesh Kumar. 2020. "Caterpillar Bets on Self-driving Machines Impervious to Pandemics." (12 October 2020), *Reuters*. <www.reuters.com/article/idUSKBN26X1ET>. (Accessed 20 November 2021).

Sykes, Nathan. 2018. "How Manufacturing Automation Is Evolving." (7 March 2018), *Robotics Business Review*. <www.roboticsbusinessreview.com/manufacturing/how-manufacturing-automation-is-evolving/>. (Accessed 9 January 2021).

U.S. Bureau of Labor Statistics. 2021. "Industries at a Glance: Manufacturing: NAICS 31–33." (8 January 2021), *U.S. Department of Labor, Bureau of Labor Statistics*. <www.bls.gov/iag/tgs/iag31-33.htm>. (Accessed 10 January 2021).

Chapter 5

Abrams, Michael. 2017. "6 Paths to the Automated Construction Site." (8 November 2017), *American Society of Mechanical Engineers*. <www.asme.org/topics-resources/content/6-paths-automated-construction-site>. (Accessed 9 January 2021).

Armstrong Siddeley Heritage Trust. 2019. "A Brief History of W. G. Armstrong." *Armstrong Siddeley Heritage Trust*. <www.armstrongsiddeleyheritagetrust.com/armstrong-master>. (Accessed 22 November 2021).

Brownell, Blaine. 2019. "Hybrid Technologies and the Automation of Construction." (24 October 2019), *Architect Magazine.* <www.architectmagazine.com/technology/ hybrid-technologies-and-the-automation-of-construction_o>. (Accessed 9 January 2021).

Ceccarelli, Marco. 2020. "Design and Reconstruction of an Ancient Roman Crane." (8 December 2020), *Advances in Historical Studies*, 9: 261–283. <https://doi. org/10.4236/ahs.2020.95021>.

Chea, Cheav Por et al. 2020. "An Integrated Review of Automation and Robotic Technologies for Structural Prefabrication and Construction." (29 May 2020), *Transportation Safety and Environment*, 2, no. 2: 81–96. <https://doi. org/10.1093/tse/tdaa007>.

Cutieru, Andreea. 2020. "An Overview of Digital Fabrication in Architecture." (29 May 2020), *ArchDaily.* <www.archdaily.com/940530/an-overview-of-digital- fabrication-in-architecture?ad_medium=widget&ad_name=related-article&ad_ content=945761>. (Accessed 9 January 2021).

Encyclopaedia Britannica. "William George Armstrong, Baron Armstrong." *Encyclopaedia Britannica.* <www.britannica.com/biography/William-George- Armstrong-Baron-Armstrong-of-Cragside>. (Accessed 22 November 2021).

Fischer, Martin, and Oussama Khatib. 2019. "Leveraging Human-Robot Collaboration in Construction." Summary for CIFE Seed Proposals for Academic Year 2019– 20. *Stanford University, Center for Integrated Facility Engineering.* <https://cife. stanford.edu/Seed2019%20HumanRobotCollaboration>.

Gordon, Rachel. 2019. "Self-transforming Robot Blocks Jump, Spin, Flip, and Identify Each Other." (30 October 2019), *MIT News.* <https://news.mit.edu/ 2019/self-transforming-robot-blocks-jump-spin-flip-identify-each-other-1030>. (Accessed 22 November 2021).

Grossman, David. 2019. "This Company Turns Old Excavators and Bulldozers Into Smart Machines: But the Robots Aren't Gunning for Construction Workers' Jobs." (28 September 2019), *Popular Mechanics.* <www.popularmechanics. com/technology/infrastructure/a29131330/automated-construction-equipment/>. (Accessed 9 January 2021).

Hasegawa, Yukio. 2000. "A New Wave of Construction Automation and Robotics in Japan." 2000 Proceedings of the 17th International Symposium on Automation and Robotics in Construction. <www.iaarc.org/publications/proceedings_of_ the_17th_isarc/open_issues_and_future_possibilities_in_the_eu_construction_ automation.html>.

Hasegawa, Yukio. 2006. "Construction Automation and Robotics in the 21st Century." 2006 Proceedings of the 23rd International Symposium on Automation and Robotics in Construction. <www.iaarc.org/publications/ proceedings_of_the_23rd_isarc/construction_automation_and_robotics_in_ the_21st_century.html>.

Hutson, Matthew. 2018. "Here's What the Future of Haptic Technology Looks (or Rather, Feels) Like." (28 December 2018), *Smithsonian Magazine.* <www. smithsonianmag.com/innovation/heres-what-future-haptic-technology-looks- or-rather-feels-180971097/>. (Accessed 22 November 2021).

Koskela, Lauri. 1992. "Process Improvement and Automation in Construction: Opposing or Complementing Approaches?" The 9th International Symposium on Automation and Robotics in Construction, 3–5 June 1992. <http://citeseerx. ist.psu.edu/viewdoc/download;jsessionid=9813028469C36E98EB4FB0D60E7E2 55A?doi=10.1.1.658.9633&rep=rep1&type=pdf>.

Lau, Darwin. 2020. "A Fully Automated Construction Industry? Still a Long Road Ahead." (22 August 2020), *ArchDaily*. <www.archdaily.com/945761/a-fully-automated-construction-industry-still-a-long-road-ahead>. (Accessed 9 January 2021).

McCaslin. 2018. "High Points in the History of Construction Machinery." (19 December 2018), *Texas Final Drive*. <http://info.texasfinaldrive.com/shop-talk-blog/high-points-in-the-history-of-construction-machinery>. (Accessed 9 January 2021).

McCaslin. 2018. "William Otis: Grandfather of the Hydraulic Excavator." (24 May 2018), *Texas Final Drive*. <https://info.texasfinaldrive.com/shop-talk-blog/william-otis-grandfather-of-the-hydraulic-excavator>. (Accessed 22 November 2021).

McFadden, Christopher. 2020. "9 Major Milestones in the Evolution of Heavy Construction Equipment." (2 June 2020), *Interesting Engineering*. <https:// interestingengineering.com/9-major-milestones-in-the-evolution-of-heavy-construction-equipment>. (Accessed 9 January 2021).

Mining Foundation of the Southwest. "William Smith Otis: 2012 Inductee from Mining's Past." *Mining Foundation of the Southwest*. <www.miningfoundationsw. org/William_Otis>. (Accessed 22 November 2021).

Moore, Sam. 2017. "William Otis and the Steam Shovel." (3 April 2017), *Farm Collector*. <www.farmcollector.com/equipment/steam-shovels-zmlz17may zhur/>. (Accessed 22 November 2021).

Ng, Chun Lun Otto. 2011. "Project WallBots." (Fall 2011), *MIT Architecture*. <https://architecture.mit.edu/architecture-and-urbanism/project/wallbots>. (Accessed 22 November 2021).

Skibniewski, Miroslaw J. 1992. "Current Status of Construction Automation and Robotics in the United States of America." The 9th International Symposium on Automation and Robotics in Construction, 3–5 June 1992. <http://citeseerx. ist.psu.edu/viewdoc/download?doi=10.1.1.458.8373&rep=rep1&type=pdf>.

U.S. Bureau of Labor Statistics. 2021. "Industries at a Glance: Construction: NAICS 23." (8 January 2021), *U.S. Department of Labor, Bureau of Labor Statistics*. <www.bls.gov/iag/tgs/iag23.htm>. (Accessed 10 January 2021).

Chapter 6

Allen, J. M. 2019. "History of Reed Ships." (Compiled 28 February 2010, Updated July 2019), *atlantisbolivia.org*. <www.atlantisbolivia.org/areedboathistory. htm>. (Accessed 23 November 2021).

Association of American Railroads. 2020. "Freight Railroads and Positive Train Control (PTC)." Fact Sheet, August 2020. <www.aar.org/wp-content/uploads/2020/08/AAR-PTC-Fact-Sheet.pdf>. (Accessed 9 January 2021).

Association of American Railroads. 2020. "How Technology Drives the Future of Rail." (November 2020). <www.aar.org/article/the-future-of-rail/#!>. (Accessed 9 January 2021).

Auer, Ashley, Shelley Feese, and Stephen Lockwood. 2016. "History of Intelligent Transportation Systems." Report produced by Booz Allen Hamilton, FHWA-JPO-16–329, May 2016. *U.S. Department of Transportation, Intelligent Transportation Systems Joint Program Office.* <www.itsga.org/wp-content/uploads/2016/08/ITS-JPO-History-of-ITS.pdf>.

Banker, Steve. 2019. "Ryder Uses Robotic Process Automation To Automate Transportation Planning." (1 June 2019), *Forbes.* <www.forbes.com/sites/stevebanker/2019/06/01/ryder-uses-robotic-process-automation-to-automate-transportation-planning/?sh=2737dae8781e>. (Accessed 9 January 2021).

Blitz, Matt. 2016. "Movin' On Up: The Curious Birth and Rapid Rise of the Escalator." (6 April 2016), *Popular Mechanics.* <www.popularmechanics.com/technology/gadgets/a20291/moving-on-up-the-escalato>. (Accessed 23 November 2021).

Cottrell, Wayne D. 2015. "A Very Brief History of Automation in Transportation." (6 October 2015), *ATRA.* <www.advancedtransit.org/library/news/a-very-brief-history-of-automation-in-transportation/>. (Accessed 9 January 2021).

Daher, Michael et al. 2019. "How Are Global Shippers Evolving to Meet Tomorrow's Demand? The Future of the Movement of Goods." *Deloitte Insights.* <https://www2.deloitte.com/us/en/insights/focus/future-of-mobility/future-of-freight-connected-data-intelligent-automation.html>.

Davis, River, and Tsuyoshi Inajima. 2021. "First Autonomous Cargo Ship Faces Test With 236-Mile Voyage." (30 August 2021), *Bloomberg.* <www.bloomberg.com/news/articles/2021-08-30/first-autonomous-cargo-ship-faces-test-with-236-mile-voyage?sref=P6Q0mxvj>. (Accessed 24 November 2021).

Drents Museum. 2016. "The Pesse Canoe." *Drents Museum.* <https://drentsmuseum.nl/en/in-the-spotlight-top-exhibits/pesse-canoe>. (Accessed 23 November 2021).

Federal Railroad Administration. 2021. "Positive Train Control (PTC)." (9 September 2021), *U.S. Department of Transportation, Federal Railroad Administration.* <https://railroads.dot.gov/train-control/ptc/positive-train-control-ptc>. (Accessed 24 November 2021).

Gittleman, Maury, and Kristen Monaco. 2019. "Automation Isn't About to Make Truckers Obsolete." (18 September 2019), *Harvard Business Review.* <https://hbr.org/2019/09/automation-isnt-about-to-make-truckers-obsolete>. (Accessed 9 January 2019).

Godavarthy, Ranjit. 2019. "Transit Automation Technologies: A Review of Transit Agency Perspective." Report produced by North Dakota State University, Upper Great Plains Transportation Institute, Small Urban and Rural Transit Center, December 2019. *U.S. Department of Transportation.* <www.ugpti.org/resources/reports/details.php?id=978>.

Hancock, P. A., Illah Nourbakhsh, and Jack Stewart. 2019. "On the Future of Transportation in an Era of Automated and Autonomous Vehicles." (16 April 2019), *PNAS*, 116, no. 16: 7684–7691. <https://doi.org/10.1073/pnas.1805770115>.

Hodge, Lawrence. 2021. "Two Autonomous Cargo Ships Are about to Set Sail." (1 September 2021), *Jalopnik.* <https://jalopnik.com/two-autonomous-cargo-ships-are-about-to-set-sail-1847591029>. (Accessed 24 November 2021).

Klesty, Victoria. 2021. "Yara Debuts World's First Autonomous Electric Container Ship." (19 November 2021), *Reuters.* <www.reuters.com/markets/europe/yara-debuts-worlds-first-autonomous-electric-container-ship-2021-11-19/>. (Accessed 24 November 2021).

McFadden, Christopher. 2021. "Autonomous Planes – When Will They Get Flight Clearance? Will We See a Future Without Pilots? Let's Take a Quick Look." (31 October 2021), *Interesting Engineering.* <https://interestingengineering.com/will-autonomous-planes-get-flight-clearance>. (Accessed 24 November 2021).

Migiro, Geoffrey. 2018. "The Oldest Ships In The World." (21 May 2018), *WorldAtlas.* <www.worldatlas.com/articles/the-oldest-ships-in-the-world.html>. (Accessed 23 November 2021).

Paleja, Ameya. 2021. "World's First Autonomous Electric Container Ship Completed Its First Trip: And It Will Save 1,000 Tons of Carbon Emissions a Year." (22 November 2021), *Interesting Engineering.* <https://interestingengineering.com/worlds-first-autonomous-electric-container-ship-completed-its-first-trip>. (Accessed 24 November 2021).

Union Pacific. "Positive Train Control." <www.up.com/media/media_kit/ptc/about-ptc/>. (Accessed 24 November 2021).

U.S. Bureau of Labor Statistics. 2021. "Industries at a Glance: Transportation and Warehousing: NAICS 48–49." (8 January 2021), *U.S. Department of Labor, Bureau of Labor Statistics.* <www.bls.gov/iag/tgs/iag48-49.htm>. (Accessed 10 January 2021).

U.S. Government Accountability Office. 2019. "Automated Trucking: Federal Agencies Should Take Additional Steps to Prepare for Potential Workforce Effects." Report to the Subcommittee on Transportation, Housing and Urban Development, and Related Agencies, Committee on Appropriations, U.S. Senate, GAO-19–161, March 2019. *U.S. Government Accountability Office.*

U.S. Government Accountability Office. 2017. "Automated Vehicles: Comprehensive Plan Could Help DOT Address Challenges." Report to Congressional Committees, GAO-18–132, November 2017. *U.S. Government Accountability Office.*

Viegas, José. 2017. "Automation and the Future of Public Transport." (24 February 2017), *Intelligent Transport.* <www.intelligenttransport.com/transport-articles/72914/automation-future-public-transport/>. (Accessed 9 January 2021).

Yara International. 2021. "Yara to Start Operating the World's First Fully Emission-free Container Ship." Corporate Press Release, 19 November 2021. *Yara International.* <www.yara.com/corporate-releases/yara-to-start-operating-the-worlds-first-fully-emission-free-container-ship/>.

Chapter 7

Ambrosino, Brandon. 2014. "Why the Disappearance of Hotel Room Keys Marks the End of Hospitality." (18 February 2014), *Quartz*. <https://qz.com/177505/why-the-disappearance-of-hotel-room-keys-marks-the-end-of-hospitality/>. (Accessed 26 November 2021).

Attala, John. 2019. "10 Ways Smart Technology is Reshaping the Hotel Industry." (25 March 2019), *Hotel Management*. <www.hotelmanagement.net/tech/10-ways-smart-technology-reshaping-hotel-industry>. (Accessed 9 January 2021).

Beck, Tony. 2007. "Barron's Lock." *The Lock Collectors Association*. <www.lockcollectors.eu/members/lockdatabase/bar1/_index.htm>. (Accessed 26 November 2021).

Bellis, Mary. 2019. "The History of Vending Machines: The First Recorded Machine Provided Holy Water in Temples." (3 December 2019), *ThoughtCo*. <www.thoughtco.com/the-history-of-vending-machines-1992599>. (Accessed 27 November 2021).

Cohen, Aaron. 2018. "Robots Are Making Our Restaurants Safer." (19 December 2018), *Modern Restaurant Management*. <https://modernrestaurantmanagement.com/robots-are-making-our-restaurants-safer/>. (Accessed 9 January 2021).

Cox, Erik. 2019. "Will Restaurant Automation Solve the Industry's Labor Problem?" (10 May 2019), *Modern Restaurant Management*. <https://modernrestaurantmanagement.com/will-restaurant-automation-solve-the-industrys-labor-problem/>. (Accessed 9 January 2021).

Davis, Kenrick. 2020. "Welcome to China's Latest 'Robot Restaurant'." (1 July 2020), *World Economic Forum*. <www.weforum.org/agenda/2020/07/china-robots-ai-restaurant-hospitality>. (Accessed 9 January 2021).

Fromm, Walter. 1974. "Magnetic Door Lock System." Filed 15 May 1974, Application No. 470,188. Patent No. 3,919,869, 18 November 1975. *U.S. Patent and Trademark Office*.

Fruen, William Henry. 1884. "Automatic Liquid-Drawing Device." Specification forming part of Letters Patent No. 309,219, 16 December 1884. *U.S. Patent Office*.

Guinness World Records. "Oldest Hotel." *Guinness World Records*. <www.guinnessworldrecords.com/world-records/oldest-hotel/>. (Accessed 26 November 2021).

Hahling, Charles. 1929. "Bottle Vending Machine." Application filed 4 November 1929, Serial No. 404,672. Patent No. 1,809,693, 9 June 1931. *U.S. Patent Office*.

Hennessy, Maggie. 2018. "Inside the Rise of Restaurant Automation." (September 2018), *FSR*. <www.fsrmagazine.com/research/inside-rise-restaurant-automation>. (Accessed 9 January 2021).

Hollander, Catherine. 2014. "A History of Vending Machines, From Chewing Gum to 90-Second Pasta." (4 April 2014), *Bon Appétit*. <www.bonappetit.com/entertaining-style/trends-news/slideshow/history-vending-machine>. (Accessed 27 November 2021).

Jane Austen Centre. "Joseph Bramah: Inventor Extraordinaire." *JaneAusten.co.uk*. <https://janeausten.co.uk/blogs/authors-artists-vagrants/joseph-bramah-inventor-extraordinaire>. (Accessed 26 November 2021).

Joshi, Naveen. 2020. "Bon Appétit! Robotic Restaurants Are The Future." (3 February 2020), *Forbes*. <www.forbes.com/sites/cognitiveworld/2020/02/03/bon-apptit-robotic-restaurants-are-the-future/?utm_source=facebook&utm_medium=social&utm_term=&utm_content=&utm_campaign=ypoedge&sh=1e23c6252136>. (Accessed 9 January 2021).

Kastner, Jeffrey. 2006. "National Insecurity: A. C. Hobbs and the Great Lock Controversy of 1851." (Summer 2006), *Cabinet*. <https://cabinetmagazine.org/issues/22/kastner.php>. (Accessed 26 November 2021).

Lally, Bill. 2018. "Automation is the Future of Hotels." (5 March 2018), *Today's Hotelier*. <www.todayshotelier.com/2018/03/05/automation-is-the-future-of-hotels/>. (Accessed 9 January 2021).

Levy-Bonvin, Jacques. 2003. "Hotels | A Brief History." (15 December 2003), *Hospitality Net*. <www.hospitalitynet.org/opinion/4017990.html>. (Accessed 9 January 2021).

MessyNessy. 2017. "Oh to Have Eaten at the Automat, Just Once." (4 August 2017), *Cabinet of Chic Curiosities*. <www.messynessychic.com/2017/08/04/oh-to-have-eaten-at-the-automat-just-once/>. (Accessed 26 November 2021).

Propst, Robert L. 1981. "Locking System Using Codable Magnetic Cards." Filed 12 May 1981, Application No. 262,841. Patent No. 4,409,806, 18 October 1983. *U.S. Patent and Trademark Office*.

Romano, Andrea. 2018. "The World's Oldest Hotel Has Been in the Same Family for 52 Generations (Video)." (10 August 2018), *Travel + Leisure*. <www.travelandleisure.com/hotels-resorts/japanese-hotel-oldest-in-the-world>. (Accessed 26 November 2021).

Russell and Dawson. "Evolution of Hospitality Industry." *Russell and Dawson*. <www.rdaep.com/blogs/evolution-hospitality-industry/>. (Accessed 26 November 2021).

Sabatini, Katie. 2019. "Automation Innovation: Cobots and Other Technologies for Your Kitchen." *Nutrition and Foodservice Edge*, July–August 2019. <www.anfponline.org/docs/default-source/legacy-docs/docs/ce-articles/fpc072019.pdf>.

Schlage, Ernest L. 1964. "Magnetic Locking Device and Method of Combinating the Same." Filed 14 July 1964, Serial No. 382,548. Patent No. 3,271,983, 13 September 1966. *U.S. Patent Office*.

Sherman, George W. 1894. "Vending Apparatus." Specification forming part of Letters Patent No. 511,865, 2 January 1894. *U.S. Patent Office*.

Sornes, Tor. 1978. "Lock Arrangement Employing Mechanically Acting Code Card and Key Card." Filed 28 March 1978, Application No. 891,390. Patent No. 4,149,394, 17 April 1979. *U.S. Patent and Trademark Office*.

Starkov, Max. 2020. "Is Hospitality Ready for the Army of Robots Coming to a Hotel Near You?" (11 December 2020), *Hospitality Net*. <www.hospitalitynet.org/opinion/4102065.html>. (Accessed 9 January 2021).

Strauss, Bob. 2021. "The Rise and Fall of the Automat: Whatever Happened to Horn and Hardart?" (31 January 2021), *ThoughtCo.* <www.thoughtco.com/the-rise-and-fall-of-the-automat-4152992>. (Accessed 26 November 2021).

U.S. Bureau of Labor Statistics. 2021. "Industries at a Glance: Accommodation and Food Services: NAICS 72." (8 January 2021), *U.S. Department of Labor, Bureau of Labor Statistics.* <www.bls.gov/iag/tgs/iag72.htm>. (Accessed 10 January 2021).

Weir, William. 2009. "History of the Cafeteria." (9 December 2009), *Hartford Courant.* <www.courant.com/news/connecticut/hc-xpm-2009-12-09-09120 812523134-story.html>. (Accessed 27 November 2021).

Wich, Samuel. "The Origins of the Hospitality Industry and What Lies Ahead." *EHL Insights.* <https://hospitalityinsights.ehl.edu/origins-hospitality-industry>. (Accessed 26 November 2021).

Williams, Court. 2018. "The Growing Use of Technology and Robotics in Food Service." (6 April 2018), *Hospitality Net.* <www.hospitalitynet.org/opinion/4087781.html>. (Accessed 9 January 2021).

Wolfe, Anna. 2019. "3 Reasons Automation Is Redefining Restaurants." (18 October 2019), *Hospitality Technology.* <https://hospitalitytech.com/3-reasons-automation-redefining-restaurants>. (Accessed 9 January 2021).

Yale, Linus, Jr. 1863. "Improvement in Locks." Specification forming part of Letters Patent No. 1,326, Reissue No. 1,470, 28 April 1863. *U.S. Patent Office.*

Yale, Linus, Jr. 1863. "Improvement in Locks." Specification forming part of Letters Patent No. 32,331, Reissue No. 1,469, 28 April 1863. *U.S. Patent Office.*

Yale, Linus, Jr. 1861. "Lock." Specification of Letters Patent No. 31,278, 29 January 1861. *U.S. Patent Office.*

Chapter 8

Bell, Alexander Graham. 1876. "Improvement in Telegraphy." Specification forming part of Letters Patent No. 174,465, 7 March 1876. *U.S. Patent Office.*

Brooks, Ashley. 2015. "Health Information Management History: Past, Present and Future." (23 March 2015), *Rasmussen University.* <www.rasmussen.edu/degrees/health-sciences/blog/health-information-management-history/>. (Accessed 28 November 2021).

Felder, Robin. 2003. "Medical Automation – A Technologically Enhanced Work Environment to Reduce the Burden of Care on Nursing Staff and a Solution to the Health Care Cost Crisis." (May–June 2003), *Nursing Outlook*, 51, no. 3: S5–S10. <https://doi.org/10.1016/S0029-6554(03)00102-7>.

Field, Marilyn J., editor. 1996. *Telemedicine: A Guide to Assessing Telecommunications in Health Care.* Washington, DC: National Academy Press.

Hillman, Dan. 2020. "The Role of Intelligent Automation in Reducing Waste and Improving Efficiency in the Revenue Cycle." (4 February 2020), *Healthcare Financial Management Association.* <www.hfma.org/topics/hfm/2020/february/the-role-of-intelligent-automation-in-reducing-waste-and-improvi.html>. (Accessed 9 January 2021).

Industry Council for Emergency Response Technologies and 911 Education Foundation. "History of 911: And What It Means for the Future of Emergency Communications." <https://static.wixstatic.com/ugd/b8d2ce_e6b60db90b47454 dbb047f451278aa66.pdf>. (Accessed 28 November 2021).

National 911 Program. "The National 911 Program Celebrates 50 Years of 911." *National Highway Traffic Safety Administration, Office of Emergency Medical Services.* <www.911.gov/50-years-of-911.html>. (Accessed 28 November 2021).

National Emergency Number Association. "9–1–1 Origin and History." <www.nena.org/page/911overviewfacts>. (Accessed 28 November 2021).

Overstreet, Kim. 2021. "Med Device Market Shifting Business Models to Automation and Technology." (4 January 2021), *OEM.* <www.oemmagazine.org/home/article/21219674/med-device-market-shifting-business-models-to-automation-and-technology>. (Accessed 9 January 2021).

Rampton, Vanessa, Maria Böhmer, and Anita Winkler. 2021. "Medical Technologies Past and Present: How History Helps to Understand the Digital Era." (7 July 2021), *Journal of Medical Humanities.* <https://doi.org/10.1007/s10912-021-09699-x>.

Schmidt, Christine K. et al. 2020. "Engineering Microrobots for Targeted Cancer Therapies from a Medical Perspective." (5 November 2020), *Nature Communications*, 11. <https://doi.org/10.1038/s41467-020-19322-7>.

Smith, Clarice. 2018. "Robotic Process Automation and Health Informatics and Information Management." (6 November 2018), *Journal of AHIMA.* <https://journal.ahima.org/robotic-process-automation-and-health-informatics-and-information-management/>. (Accessed 9 January 2021).

Studdiford, James S. et al. 1996. "The Telephone in Primary Care." (March 1996), *Primary Care: Clinics in Office Practice*, 23, no. 1: 83–98. <https://doi.org/10.1016/S0095-4543(05)70262-1>.

Thede, Linda Q., and Jeanne P. Sewell. 2012. "Computer Development and Health Care Information Systems 1950 to Present." (8 December 2012). <http://dlthede.net/informatics/chap01introni/healthcare_computers.html>. (Accessed 28 November 2021).

Tripathi, Micky. 2012. "EHR Evolution: Policy and Legislation Forces Changing the EHR." (October 2012), *Journal of AHIMA*, 83, no. 10: 24–29. <https://library.ahima.org/doc?oid=105689>.

Turgeon, Philippe et al. 2020. "Mechanical Design of a New Device to Assist Eating in People with Movement Disorders." (13 March 2020), *Assistive Technology.* <https://doi.org/10.1080/10400435.2020.1734111>.

U.S. Bureau of Labor Statistics. 2021. "Industries at a Glance: Health Care and Social Assistance: NAICS 62." (8 January 2021), *U.S. Department of Labor, Bureau of Labor Statistics.* <www.bls.gov/iag/tgs/iag62.htm>. (Accessed 10 January 2021).

Webster, Thomas J. 2006. "Nanomedicine: What's in a Definition?" (June 2006), *International Journal of Nanomedicine*, 1, no. 2: 115–116. <https://doi.org/10.2147/nano.2006.1.2.115>.

Weenk, Mariska et al. 2018. "A Smart All-in-one Device to Measure Vital Signs in Admitted Patients." (12 February 2018), *PLoS ONE*, 13, no. 2. <https://doi.org/10.1371/journal.pone.0190138>.

Willis, Matthew et al. 2019. "The Future of Health Care: Protocol for Measuring the Potential of Task Automation Grounded in the National Health Service Primary Care System." (9 April 2019), *JMIR Research Protocols*, 8, no. 4. <www.ncbi.nlm.nih.gov/pmc/articles/PMC6477572/>.

Willis, Matthew et al. 2020. "Qualitative and Quantitative Approach to Assess the Potential for Automating Administrative Tasks in General Practice." (8 June 2020), *BMJ Open*, 10, no. 6. <https://doi.org/10.1136/bmjopen-2019-032412>.

Yeager, Andrew. 2018. "How a Small Alabama Town Pioneered the First 9–1–1 Call." (21 February 2018), *Public Radio WBHM 90.3 FM*. <https://wbhm.org/2018/how-a-small-alabama-town-pioneered-the-first-9-1-1-call/>. (Accessed 28 November 2021).

Chapter 9

Alexander, Heidi S. 2019. "Easy Automation: Automating Certain Tasks Can Save You Time and Expand Your Practice." (1 July 2019), *American Bar Association*. <www.americanbar.org/groups/law_practice/publications/law_practice_magazine/2019/JA2019/JA19Alexander/>. (Accessed 10 January 2021).

Beaulieu, Raphaël. "Automation and the Future of Legal Drafting Technology." *SCL Student Bytes*. <https://bytes.scl.org/automation-and-the-future-of-legal-drafting-technology/>. (Accessed 10 January 2021).

Dowling, Stephen. 2020. "The Cheap Pen That Changed Writing Forever." (29 October 2020), *BBC*. <www.bbc.com/future/article/20201028-history-of-the-ballpoint-pen>. (Accessed 29 November 2021).

Fidler, Devin. 2015. "Here's How Managers Can Be Replaced by Software." (21 April 2015), *Harvard Business Review*. <https://hbr.org/2015/04/heres-how-managers-can-be-replaced-by-software>. (Accessed 10 January 2021).

Gurchiek, Kathy. "Human-looking Robots Entering the Workplace." *SHRM*. <www.shrm.org/hr-today/news/hr-news/pages/cms_019627.aspx>. (Accessed 10 January 2021).

Henley, Barron K. 2018. "Technology Tools for Real Property and Trusts and Estates Lawyers: A Range of Technology Tools Designed to Assist RPTE Lawyers Are Discussed." (November–December 2018), *American Bar Association*. <www.americanbar.org/groups/real_property_trust_estate/publications/probate-property-magazine/2018/november-december-2018/technology-tools-real-property-and-trusts-and-estates-lawyers/>. (Accessed 10 January 2021).

IBM Education Department. 1949. "The History of IBM Electric Typewriters." *IBM*. <www.ibm.com/ibm/history/exhibits/modelb/modelb_history.html>. (Accessed 29 November 2021).

Johnsen, Edwin G., editor. 1976. *Automation Technology Applied to Public Service*. Washington, DC: U.S. Department of Commerce, National Bureau of Standards. <https://nvlpubs.nist.gov/nistpubs/Legacy/SP/nbsspecialpublication448.pdf>.

Kellman, Ryan, Elissa Nadworny, and Adam Cole. 2016. "Trace the Remarkable History of the Humble Pencil." (11 October 2016), *NPR*. <www.npr.org/sections/ed/2016/10/11/492999969/origin-of-pencil-lead>. (Accessed 29 November 2021).

Lewis, Nicole. 2020. "Using Robots in the Coronavirus Era." (28 April 2020), *SHRM*. <www.shrm.org/resourcesandtools/hr-topics/technology/pages/using-robots-coronavirus-era.aspx>. (Accessed 10 January 2021).

Rashid, Mohammad A., Liaquat Hossain, and Jon David Patrick. 2002. "The Evolution of ERP Systems: A Historical Perspective." In *Enterprise Resource Planning: Global Opportunities and Challenges,* edited by Hossain, Liaquat, Jon David Patrick, and Mohammad A. Rashid, 1–16. Hershey, PA: IGI Global. <https://doi.org/10.4018/978-1-931777-06-3.ch001>.

Records, Hal et al. 2007. "The Potential Impact of Speech Recognition Technology on Workplace Productivity." *Issues in Information Systems*, VIII, no. 2: 541–546. <https://doi.org/10.48009/2_iis_2007_541-546>.

Rubin, Arthur. 1983. *The Automated Office: An Environment for Productive Work, or an Information Factory? Executive Summary*. Washington, DC: U.S. Department of Commerce, National Bureau of Standards. <https://nvlpubs.nist.gov/nistpubs/Legacy/IR/nbsir83-2784-2.pdf>.

Rynkiewicz, Stephen. 2018. "Best Speech Recognition Software? Market Dictates One Choice." (10 March 2018), *American Bar Association*. <www.abajournal.com/news/article/best_speech_recognition_software/?utm_source=maestro&utm_medium=email&utm_campaign=tech_monthly>. (Accessed 10 January 2021).

Shah, Kevin. 2020. "A Brief History Of Pens: The Story of One of the Most Underrated Inventions of Mankind." (26 June 2020), *Medium*. <https://historyofyesterday.com/a-brief-history-of-pens-7f6666d4446d>. (Accessed 29 November 2021).

Smithsonian Education. 1998. "Carbons to Computers: Typewriters." *Smithsonian Institution*. <www.smithsonianeducation.org/scitech/carbons/typewriters.html>. (Accessed 29 November 2021).

Tancia Ltd. 2016. "The History of the Pencil." (9 September 2016). <www.pens.co.uk/pen2paper/wp-content/uploads/2016/09/The-History-of-the-Pencil.pdf>. (Accessed 29 November 2021).

Thomson, Piper. 2020. "The Complete History of ERP: Its Rise to a Powerful Solution." (23 January 2020), *G2*. <www.g2.com/articles/history-of-erp>. (Accessed 29 November 2021).

Tobenkin, David. 2019. "HR Needs to Stay Ahead of Automation: Harness the Power of Automation or Risk Being Automated Out of Your HR Job." (26 February 2019), *SHRM*. <www.shrm.org/hr-today/news/hr-magazine/spring2019/pages/hr-needs-to-stay-ahead-of-automation.aspx>. (Accessed 10 January 2021).

U.S. Bureau of Labor Statistics. 2021. "Industries at a Glance: Administrative and Support and Waste Management and Remediation Services: NAICS 56." (8 January 2021), *U.S. Department of Labor, Bureau of Labor Statistics*. <www.bls.gov/iag/tgs/iag56.htm>. (Accessed 10 January 2021).

Zielinski, Dave. 2019. "HR and Voice Recognition Technology: HR Industry Vendors Have Started Moving Their Voice-activated Applications into Real-world Use." (28 August 2019), *SHRM*. <www.shrm.org/hr-today/news/hr-magazine/fall2019/pages/hr-and-voice-recognition-technology.aspx>. (Accessed 10 January 2021).

Zunenshine, Michael. 2020. "14 Best Voice Recognition Software for Speech Dictation 2020." (1 October 2020), *CRM.org*. <https://crm.org/news/best-voice-recognition-software>. (Accessed 10 January 2021).

Chapter 10

Barshay, Jill for the Hechinger Report. 2013. "Q&A With Knewton's David Kuntz, Maker of Algorithms That Replace Some Teacher Work." (July 2013), *Wired*. <www.wired.com/insights/2013/07/qa-with-knewtons-david-kuntz-maker-of-algorithms-that-replace-some-teacher-work/>. (Accessed 10 January 2021).

Bidshahri, Raya. 2017. "Why Education Is the Hardest Sector of the Economy to Automate." (13 August 2017), *Singularity Hub*. <https://singularityhub.com/2017/08/13/why-education-is-the-hardest-sector-of-the-economy-to-automate/>. (Accessed 10 January 2021).

Bryant, Jake et al. 2020. "How Artificial Intelligence Will Impact K-12 Teachers." (14 January 2020), *McKinsey and Company*. <www.mckinsey.com/industries/public-and-social-sector/our-insights/how-artificial-intelligence-will-impact-k-12-teachers>.

Center for Children and Technology. 2004. "Television Goes to School: The Impact of Video on Student Learning in Formal Education." (January 2004), *Corporation for Public Broadcasting*. <https://dcmp.org/learn/static-assets/nadh173.pdf>.

Dikli, Semire. 2006. "An Overview of Automated Scoring of Essays." (August 2006), *Journal of Technology, Learning, and Assessment*, 5, no. 1. <https://files.eric.ed.gov/fulltext/EJ843855.pdf>.

Ediger, Marlow. 1999. "Joseph Lancaster and the History of Reading Instruction." ERIC No. ED432004, 17 August 1999. *Educational Resources Information Center (ERIC)*. U.S. Department of Education, Office of Educational Research and Improvement. <https://eric.ed.gov/?id=ED432004>.

Educause Learning Initiative. 2017. "ELI 7 Things You Should Know about Adaptive Learning." (January 2017), *EDUCAUSE*. <https://library.educause.edu/-/media/files/library/2017/1/eli7140.pdf>.

Hanson, Charles C., and Michael Sokolski. 1967. "Photoelectric Sensing Apparatus." Filed 26 April 1967, Serial No. 633,880. Patent No. 3,518,440, 30 June 1970. *U.S. Patent Office*.

Haran, Michael. 2015. "A History of Education Technology." (29 May 2015), *Institute of Progressive Education and Learning*. <http://institute-of-progressive-education-and-learning.org/a-history-of-education-technology/>. (Accessed 30 November 2021).

Marr, Bernard. 2018. "How Is AI Used in Education – Real World Examples of Today and a Peek into the Future." (25 July 2018), *Forbes*. <www.forbes.com/sites/bernardmarr/2018/07/25/how-is-ai-used-in-education-real-world-examples-of-today-and-a-peek-into-the-future>. (Accessed 10 January 2021).

Moeller, Babette. 1996. "Learning from Television: A Research Review." CCT Reports, Issue No. 11, October 1996. *Education Development Center, Center for Children and Technology*. <http://cct.edc.org/sites/cct.edc.org/files/publications/lft_rr96.pdf>.

National Museum of American History. "Skinner Teaching Machine." *Smithsonian Institution*. <https://americanhistory.si.edu/collections/search/object/nmah_690062>. (Accessed 30 November 2021).

Ramesh, Dadi, and Suresh Kumar Sanampudi. 2021. "An Automated Essay Scoring Systems: A Systematic Literature Review." (23 September 2021), *Artificial Intelligence Review*. <https://doi.org/10.1007/s10462-021-10068-2>.

Sokolski, Michael, and Thomas J. Poole. 1974. "Test Scoring Apparatus." Filed 7 January 1974, Application No. 431,399. Patent No. 3,900,961, 26 August 1975. *U.S. Patent and Trademark Office*.

U.S. Bureau of Labor Statistics. 2021. "Industries at a Glance: Educational Services: NAICS 61." (8 January 2021), *U.S. Department of Labor, Bureau of Labor Statistics*. <www.bls.gov/iag/tgs/iag61.htm>. (Accessed 10 January 2021).

Walsh, Kelly. 2019. "Intelligent Tutoring Systems (a Decades-old Application of AI in Education)." (3 December 2019), *EmergingEdTech.com*. <www.emergingedtech.com/2019/12/intelligent-tutoring-systems-application-of-ai-in-education/>. (Accessed 4 December 2021).

Wasfy, Hatem M. et al. 2013. "The Education Sector Revolution: The Automation of Education." Paper ID No. 8044. 120th ASEE Annual Conference and Exposition, 23–26 June 2013. *American Society for Engineering Education*.

Young, Jeffrey R. 2021. "The Long and Surprising History of 'Teaching Machines'." (15 June 2021), *EdSurge*. <www.edsurge.com/news/2021-06-15-new-book-explores-the-long-and-surprising-history-of-teaching-machines>. (Accessed 30 November 2021).

Index

Printed in the United States
by Baker & Taylor Publisher Services